ZOIA BELYAKOVA

The **ROMANOVS.**
The Way It Was

Daria, Nicholas II's Forgotten Cousin

All Fell in Love with Ella

The Crimean Captives

ZOIA BELYAKOVA

The ROMANOVS.

The Way It Was

EGO PUBLISHERS
St.Petersburg

LAYOUT AND DESIGN BY
Liubov' Rakhmilevich

EDITED BY Yuri Pamfilov

PHOTOGRAPHY BY
Leonid Bogdanov

TYPE-SETTING & DESIGN BY
Veronika Rakhmilevich

COLOR CORRECTION BY
Oleg Popov (AMOS)

COLOR SEPARATION BY
AMOS (St.Petersburg)

PRINTED AND BOUND IN FINLAND
ISBN 5-8276-0034-2

Acknowledgments

This book was written, revised and rewritten over a course of three years. The work was completed thanks to the help and encouragement of my friends, associates and researchers. To them all, named and unnamed, I am sincerely grateful.

My particular, deep gratitude goes to Prince Nikita Romanov in NYC, who greatly honoured me in allowing access to family documents and with his permission to quote from unpublished letters and diaries kept in the archives of his grandmother, the Grand Duchess Xenia Alexandrovna, Hoover Institution, Stanford University, USA.

The generous assistance of Prince Nicholas Romanov is invaluable in sharing his knowledge and in allowing to view his family collection of imperial photographs.

I wish to express my gratitude to Mrs Xenia Grabbe and Mrs Maria de Pasquale, PA, USA, the living descendants of Grand Duchess Maria and Maximilian Duke of Leuchtenberg, who provided me with family records and rare illustrations.

My friends Tatiana and Boris Diedovich in San Francisco, CA, USA, graciously offered home and hospitality throughout my emotionally tiring research work at the Hoover Archives.

In St. Petersburg, thanks are also due to a number of museum experts and researchers who rendered me help in finding and handling rare pictures and photos to be used as illustrations for this book: the friendly State Hermitage administration and notably Mrs. Augusta Pobedinskaia (paintings, Russian culture department). Thanks go to the staff members of the Theatre and Music Museum and its vice-director N.Metelitsa, and to the director of the Belosselsky-Belozersky Palace and to Mrs. Maria Tzeliad for her comments and suggestions. For selecting illustrations in the prints department of the Russian National Library my gratitude is due to their experienced staff.

Mr. Alexei Shigin from the Hermitage, my co-author in quarrying information on the tragic life-story of Countess Daria Beauharnais (Duchess of Leuchtenberg), has proved to be a good friend and a colleague.

Low traditional Russian bow to all who helped to bring the book project to its close.

Foreword

Thousands of books on the Romanovs have been published both in Russia and abroad. Needless to explain why particular attention is paid today to the era of the last Tsar and the tale of "Nicholas and Alexandra". My field in research is mainly the Romanov characters whose fate remained untapped by most of the writers.

Thus, the book *Grand Duchess Maria Nikolaevna and Her Palace in St. Petersburg* (1994) for the first time highlighted the story of Nicholas I's favourite daughter and her husband Maximilian Duke of Leuchtenberg, extraordinary personalities in social and cultural life, and their descendants up to the present day. The book *Nikolaevsky Palace* (1997) recounts the story of the Grand Dukes Nikolaevichi dynastic line, many of whom held key positions in Russian history.

The present book reveals new stories of forgotten royal members and events of their lives little known to contemporary readers. The tragic destiny of Countess Daria Beauharnais, Duchess of Leuchtenberg, a second cousin of Nicholas II, is hardly known to the Russian or worldwide public.

A few books on Ella, Grand Duchess Elizabeth of Russia, were published abroad but remained unknown to Russian readers. It is truly unjust because Ella occupies a place of her own amongst the members of the Romanov dynasty being virtually unequalled and noble both in her aspirations and in her deeds. She was highly venerated by people, eventually to become a saint. She built the Martha and Mary Community of Mercy in Moscow, which remains a highlight in charitable work to the present day.

What happened to the Romanovs after the Tsar's abdication? Major details of the bloody pointless massacre of the Imperial family in Yekaterinburg have been much written about, as well as the tragedy in Alapaevsk, or the murder of Grand Duke Michael by the Bolsheviks, and the killing of the four grand dukes in the Peter and Paul fortress. However, the Court Calendar for 1917 lists 65 members of the Imperial family. Who survived, when and how? The third chapter in this book tells a tale of the Romanov captives in the Crimea in 1917–19, who miraculously escaped death.

One has to be more kind and merciful upon learning of the bygone mystery. One has to forget the fuss and vanity of the present day that is not at all our worst times. If the world is out of joint we can mend it.

St. Petersburg,
December 1999

Daria, Nicholas II's Forgotten Cousin

The world is out of joint

Shakespeare, *Hamlet*

If we were to stringently follow the strict and complex rules of dynastic delineation, then the subject of this chapter, the cousin once removed of the last Russian Emperor, has only a tenuous claim to the Romanov name. In the Court Calendar for 1917, amongst the 65 members of the Imperial family listed, we would find no mention of Countess Daria Evgenievna Beauharnais v.Leuchtenberg. She did not belong to the Imperial family in the strictest sense of the word. Nevertheless, "regal blood coursed" in her veins, as the Russian poet KR (also known as Grand Duke Constantine Constantinovich) put it. Her great-grandfather was Nicholas I, who also happened to be the great-grandfather of Nicholas II. Thus, it was this particular lady, a representative of the higher order, and a relation of the monarch, who was fated to become the "last of the Romanovs", living on in Russia another twenty years after the 1917 revolution. She became a witness to, and an unwilling participant in, the nightmare build-up of the "new world". Her fate was unique, and deserves to be heard.

Hidden away in the storage rooms of the State Hermitage are two portraits painted with an interval of sixteen years. The first is dated 1896, and is of Daria Evgenievna Kotchoubey. The second was painted in 1912, and its subject is Baroness Daria Evgenievna Grävenitz. They depict the same woman, at different periods in her life, living under different names and with different titles. In the 1920s and 1930s, this woman was known simply as Dora Evgenievna Leuchtenberg who worked in the Public Library in Leningrad.

This extraordinary woman, with her extraordinary fate, can still be regarded both as one of the Romanovs and an issue of the European royal and best aristocratic families. Her grandmother was the Grand Duchess Maria Nikolaevna, the eldest daughter of Emperor Nicholas I, who in 1839 married Maximilian Duke of Leuchtenberg. Her grandfather Maximilian Duke of Leuchtenberg was in turn the son of EugŹne Rose de Beauharnais, and the grandson of the Empress Joséphine of France, spouse of Napoleon Bonaparte. Maximilian was similarly the direct scion of the kings of Bavaria through his maternal ancestral line, his mother being Princess Augusta Amalia of Bavaria.

Daria's father, Prince Eugen Maximilianovich Romanovsky (de Beauharnais), 5th Duke of Leuchtenberg (1847–1901), was the second son of the Grand Duchess Maria and Maximilian, and he grew up in the famous Mariinsky Palace on Isaac's Square in St. Petersburg. The six surviving children in the family were granted the title Prince (Princess) Romanovsky, and enjoyed the rights of members of the Imperial House. The qualification *'Imperial Highness'* was theirs in Russia, but they had no rights to allowances from the Appanages Department. Like the other members of the Imperial family, the Leuchtenberg dukes had to swear an oath of allegiance to the autocracy on reaching twenty years of age, as well as a military oath of fealty to the Fatherland. Like the grand dukes, they had to ask for the Emperor's permission to marry, and had to select their prospective partner from the ruling dynasties of Europe.

Nevertheless, in infringement of the Statutes on the Imperial family, the elder son, Prince Nikolai Maximilianovich Romanovsky (de Beauharnais), the 4th Duke of Leuchtenberg (1843–1890), married Nadezhda S. Akinfieva (1840–1891) in 1868, who had previously been married to a colonel in the Guards regiment. The marriage was considered morganatic, and by order of Alexander II, the couple was forbidden to live in Russia. This harsh punishment didn't prevent Maria Nikolaevna's second son from making the same rash decision. In this case it was Duke Eugen Maximilianovich, who had fought in Turkestan, commanded a brigade of Uhlans in the Russo-Turkish campaigns of 1877–78, and reached the rank of a general.[1]

In 1869, Eugen entered a morganatic marriage with Daria K. Opochinina (1845–70), a granddaughter of Field Marshal M.I.Kutuzov. Needless to say the event took place abroad, in Florence. In the same year of 1869, his young spouse was granted the title of Countess de Beauharnais for herself, and for her issue, which made for a stark contrast with her relation, Nadezhda Akinfieva (née Annenkova), who had to wait eleven years in order to officially receive the title and name of her husband. In 1870, in St. Petersburg, at the Mariinsky Palace, a daughter was born and also named Daria (Dolly), after her mother who soon died following the child's difficult delivery.

Information about Dolly's childhood and youth is scarce. It is likely that many of her early years passed in the magnificent palace of her grandmother, Grand Duchess Maria Nikolaevna (at that stage the President of the Academy of Arts), with a splendid view on St Isaac's Cathedral, and the monument to her great-grandfather in the middle of the square. New information from the recently opened KGB archives reveals important and intriguing data on the life of a certain library worker, Dora Evgenievna Leuchtenberg, born in 1881 (sic), in Munich (sic), nationality – German, citizenship – Bavarian. Education: 3 years at home, probably, in the Mariinsky Palace with her widowed father; 5 years in Paris in a classical gymnasium, 2 years in Karlsruhe, where her aunt Maria Maximilianovna, Princess of Baden, could have looked after her. Then she attended the Sorbonne in Paris and a two-year course for nurses. According to the documents, she had lived only briefly in Russia, and from childhood spoke fluent German, English and French, and had a good knowledge of Italian.[2] From the documents it is not clear why Dora decided to make herself younger by eleven years, even if only on paper, effectively giving the impression that she had married aged twelve.

In 1878, Dolly's father married a second time, taking Zinaida Dmitrievna Skobeleva (1856–99), who was the sister of a prominent general and hero of the Russo-Turkish war of 1877–78, as his wife. His new spouse was only 14 years older than her foster-daughter, Dolly. In the same year, by an Imperial decree of Alexander II, Zinaida was created Countess de Beauharnais, like her step-daughter, and in 1889, by a special Imperial decree of Alexander III, Zinaida was granted the title of the Duchess of Leuchtenberg with the qualification of *Serene Highness ad personam*. Both monarchs demonstrated a willingness to shower this beauty with titles. General A.A.Mossolov wrote in his memoirs that Zina Beauharnais "was extraordinarily attractive, beautiful and joyful."[3] Grand Duke Alexander Mikhailovich admitted that describing the physical charms of this remarkable woman was entirely beyond his abilities: "I never saw anything to match her during all my trips through Europe, Asia, America and Australia, which was very lucky, as such women shouldn't be encountered too frequently."[4] There is little doubt that Zinaida was a veritable femme fatale, with a scandalous reputation, who, with royal calm, paid scant attention to infuriated gossips and the hordes of the envious.

In the diary of Tsesarevich Nicholas Alexandrovich we read: "2nd of January 1892. At half past seven I went with Sandro to Uncle Alexei's, to collect Papa and Xenia. We ate there: Aunt Miechen, Zina, Uncle Vladimir, Eugen, Alexei M. and Cyril." At Uncle Grand Duke Alexei Alexandrovich's, an intimate circle of the royal dignitaries had gathered: Emperor Alexander III, Sandro (Alexander Mikhailovich) is collecting his future wife, the Tsar's daughter Xenia; and here we find the invariable Duke Eugen with Zinaida, Vladimir, the monarch's brother, with his wife Maria Pavlovna Sr., otherwise known as Aunt Miechen, and their son Cyril [Alexei M. is probably Sandro's younger brother – Z.B.]."

In the same diary, two days later, we find: "At 6.45 went to a dress rehearsal of the opera *Esclarmonda* by Massenet. Finished at half past eleven, went to Uncle Alexei's to dine. Zina entertained us with songs."[5]

At court and amongst the nobility, Eugen was regarded as a drunkard and cuckold. The Duke's unenviable reputation was to a large extent due to the scandalous infamy of his beautiful wife Zina. Grand Duke Alexei, the Grand Admiral of the Russian Navy, had a passion for his relative Zina de Beauharnais, and the existence of this *ménage-à-trois* was common knowledge in Petersburg and Europe. This dissolute life of drink, roulette, extravagant tipping, in the notorious company of Vladimir, his wife Marie Pavlovna Sr., and Alexei, was the frequent environment of young Dolly, both in Petersburg, in the capitals of Europe, and on the Riviera.

In 1884, after the Mariinsky family palace had been sold to the Treasury to ease vast debts, Eugen and Zinaida Leuchtenberg moved to a new residence, a distinguished old mansion on the English Embankment, No.44, to which Dolly de Beauharnais returned, having completed her course at the Sorbonne.

In 1893, in Baden, Dolly married Prince Leo Mikhailovich Kotchoubey (1862–1927), an offspring of the immensely wealthy family. The Kotchoubeys were grandees, diplomats, senators, art collectors of the Ukrainian origin. Two of their children, Eugen and Natalia*, were brought up at the house on the English Embankment. In 1896, the French portrait artist François Flameng, much sought after in Petersburg, painted his portrait of beautiful Princess Dolly Kotchoubey. At about the same time, this artist produced a series of art works on the Napoleonic era, and one can imagine him jumping at the chance to paint a descendant of Joséphine de Beauharnais. (What a historical irony that Dolly was the great-granddaughter of Joséphine and Napoleon, as well as of their nemesis and conqueror, Field Marshal Kutuzov.) Strange enough is the fact that, in 1901, Eugen signed his Will and Testimony in which he mentioned his granddaughter Natalia Lvovna Kotchoubey as an heiress to a part of his assets and as an oweness to his villa

* In the Soviet period Dolly reported much later dates of their birth: 1899 and 1903.

on the Kamenny Isle, and herewith bypassing Dolly. All real estate and other property was to be inherited by his grandson, Prince Eugen Lvovich Kotchoubey, albeit "he should be annually paid only 15,000 roubles by his guardians until reaching 20-year-old age". Jewelry inherited by the young Eugen was estimated at over 1,000,000 roubles by jeweller Carl Faberge.

Little is known of the family life of the social lioness Dolly Kotchoubey, though there is no doubt that she was received in the best aristocratic salons of the capital. Right up until the First World War, St. Petersburg remained one of the most elegant and opulent capitals of Europe. True, the era of fairy-tale balls under Nicholas I and Alexander II had already passed, and the last ball in the Winter Palace was held as early as February 1903. The centre of the capital's social life and recreation became the salons of the grand dukes and other highly placed aristocrats. In all, Petersburg society had a colourful air to it, and even extravagant grand duchesses such as Maria Pavlovna, Sr., received not only divorced ladies, but even certain members of the nouveaux riches. Each of the salons led its own particular life, but Princess Dolly Kotchoubey was a welcome guest everywhere. High society during that era was made up of about ten houses. Countess Marie Kleinmichel, already approaching seventy years of age, was famed as the capital's most accomplished hostess, and she remained the heart and soul of the city's high-life, with guests ranging from diplomats and ministers to leading military officials, artists and beauties. The salon of Elizaveta (Betsy) Shuvalova became the talk of the town, following three grandiose balls. If two balls were given on the same night, guests could be left with an embarrassing choice, and scorned hosts and hostesses were left to seethe with jealousy.[6]

On the final day of the seasonal Fast in 1913, for example, a sumptuous reception was organised by Countess Betsy Shuvalova. On the same day, at the Grand Duke Vladimir's Palace on the Palace Embankment, Grand Duchess Maria was also receiving. Both houses eagerly awaited the arrival of the most prized guests, the Emperor and his elder daughters.

The Imperial family and the highest ranking guests only managed to attend Maria Pavlovna's function, in the process offending Betsy Shuvalova with their inconsiderate lack of attention. Similar occasions filled the pages of Petersburg's newspapers and magazines, and give a very accurate picture of the atmosphere of endless celebration and gaiety in which the *beau monde* of the northern capital lived.

Years passed, but Dolly continued to be noted amongst the capital's high society beauties. Yet, in 1905, she left for France, allegedly banished by Nicholas II for expressing her impartial opinions about the Emperor and his consort, a version of events, which she herself supported. When she returned, she decided to divorce Leo Kotchoubey, and did it in 1911. Her former husband and children remained at the mansion on the English Embankment.

Dora recounted a romantic version of the events leading up to her second marriage to some of her colleagues on the staff of the Public Library after the revolution. Once, when she was sailing abroad in the company of her chaperon, a battleship under the command of Captain Vladimir E. Grävenitz (1872–1916) passed by sailing in the opposite direction. The captain noticed Dolly through his binoculars and, amazed by her beauty, he signalled the steamship to halt, took a boat, came aboard to introduce himself, and finally kidnapped Dolly right from under the nose of the latter's chaperon. Their marriage took place in 1912. At first the Emperor intended to punish Grävenitz severely for taking a woman aboard a battleship. However, he forgave the captain upon learning who his wife was, and added that Grävenitz's choice was punishment enough in itself. The newlyweds settled on the English Avenue at No.26/52, and Dolly's relative, a hussar and ADC to Nicholas II, Duke Alexander G. Leuchtenberg was a neighbour, living on the same street, in a house that had been bought from the ballerina, Mathilde Kshessinskaya.

It was at this time that the artist V.K.Stember painted a portrait of Baroness Grävenitz, as mentioned earlier, providing

Countess D.E.Kotchoubey. F.Flameng. 1896. Hermitage

Mariinsky Palace
in Isaac's Square,
St. Petersburg

Maximilian
Duke of Leuchtenberg,
Dolly's grandfather.
After K.Briullov. 1849

Grand Duchess Maria Nikolaevna,
Dolly's grandmother. After 1870
Private collection, USA (first publication)

Countess D.K.Beauharnais
(née Daria Opochinina),
Dolly's mother. 1870

The Rumiantsev mansion,
44 English Embankment,
where the Kotchoubey
family lived

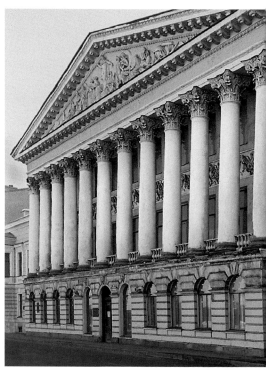

Eugen Duke
of Leuchtenberg,
Dolly's father, c. 1890

Графиня *Богарнэ*, урожд. Скобелева
Супруга Герцога Лейхтенбергскаго.
Сестра Бѣлаго Генерала М.Д. Скобелева

Countess Z.D.Beauharnais (née Skobeleva), c. 1890
Private collection, USA (first publication)

Baron
Vladimir E. Grävenitz,
Captain of
the Imperial Navy,
c. 1904

The house in the Offitserskaya St.
where the Grävenitz lived in 1912–15

The house at 63 Kamenno-ostrovsky Prospekt
where Dora lived after she divorced V.Grävenitz

Baroness D.E.Grävenitz. V.Stember. 1912. Hermitage

The house at 36 Mokhovaya St.
where Dolly and Markezetti lived until their arrest in 1937

Document from the NKVD (KGB) files

Stairs once used by Dolly and
eminent Russian writers
who worked for the *World Literature*

Grand piano in the room
that was sealed on the day
of the arrest in 1937

View of a vestibule with
an ornate lift

a visual image of this new stage in her life. Nevertheless, trouble was not far off. General Mossolov maintains that soon after the marriage, Baroness Grävenitz divorced her husband and asked his Imperial Majesty for permission to bear the title Countess Beauharnais. Permission was refused. The descendants of Baron Grävenitz believe that their ancestor Waldemar, commander of the battleship *Poltava*, committed suicide due to career problems, and was buried in Helsingfors*. The reality will perhaps never be known.

At the beginning of the First World War, Dolly began a course for nurses, as did many ladies from her circle. The receptions at palaces and stately homes, formerly famed for their balls, were indefinitely postponed, and the grand and sumptuous buildings and ballrooms were converted into makeshift hospitals and wards for the injured. At their own expense, rich ladies equipped hospital trains and medical units of nurses.

A widow and a divorcee, Dolly moved to a new luxurious apartment at No.63, Kamenno-ostrovsky Prospekt, in close proximity to her other relations, the Dukes of Leuchtenberg. It was then that she resumed her maiden name and title of Countess Beauharnais.

In January 1917, Countess D.E. Beauharnais, at her own expense, organised a medical unit of nurses and left for the Russo-Austrian front. It was there that she heard news of the revolution. According to her account, she met the revolution with sympathy, and even had a red flag hoisted in her medical unit. As is known, other members of the Romanov family demonstrated similar behaviour. In violation of both his oath as an officer, and his oath of fidelity to the autocracy given as a Grand Duke, Cyril Vladimirovich was first and only one of the grand dukes to betray his Emperor and cousin, even before the monarch's official abdication. He appeared at the Tauride Palace with a unit of Marine Guards to give an oath of allegiance

* An account given by Baron A.A.Grävenitz currently living in Brussels and St. Petersburg.

to the new Provisional Government, and hoisted a red flag over his residence to boot (13 Glinka Street). Grand Duke Nicholas Mikhailovich (Bimbo) considered the possibility of a presidential republic, and was prepared to vote as a democratic republican in the Constituent Assembly. On the eve of Nicholas II's abdication, Grand Duke Paul Alexandrovich prepared a draft project for a new constitution. It appears that they had a tendency to see the future through rose-tinted glasses, and the naive Romanovs didn't suspect the approaching tragedy.

Dolly, whose property and money remained in Petrograd, stayed at the front until October 1917. She then left for Bavaria, where she obtained Bavarian citizenship and came back ... to Russia. The mystery as to why Daria Beauharnais transformed herself into plain Dora Leuchtenberg, and, moreover, lost eleven years in age, as her new papers stated, remains unresolved. Neither is it clear what made her return to Russia, from where all her friends and relatives were leaving, or where they faced arrest and subsequent murder. When asked what her political party affiliations were, on a work application form, she replied that she was "...non-party, though of the political parties she sympathises with the Russian Communist Party (of Bolsheviks), which is why, after the revolution in Germany, she remained in Russia". On the same form it is noted that she returned to Russia "on a posting from the Austrian Red Cross of the 24th of October 1918".

Dora returned to her former apartment on Kamennoostrovsky Prospekt which by then had become a communal flat. The new inhabitants only offered to return the heaviest and most immovable furniture to her. Her bank deposits were requisitioned. She found herself alone in the wintry streets of the city. Later, Dora would recount how a certain gentleman found and took pity on her, as she lay unconscious, freezing in a snowdrift. From then on, they would be inseparable, Dora Leuchtenberg and Victor Alexandrovich Markezetti, right up until their tragic end.

An excerpt from a housing Register №12 for the Dzerzhinsky district of Leningrad, 1933:

"Leuchtenberg Dora arrived from Germany in 1918. Resides at apartment 3, No. 36 Mokhovaya St. Profession – librarian." Here on Mokhovaya, in a six-room apartment, furnished in the style of a rich stately home of a bygone era, Dora lived with her husband by a civil marriage, Victor Markezetti, and with good reason she referred to him as "Mon Victor", right up until their simultaneous arrest in the autumn of 1937.

Who was "mon Victor"? At the end of 1917, Markezetti, a major at the Austro-Hungarian army Headquarters, a former cipher clerk and head of a radio communications department, and a citizen of Austria, arrived in Moscow for the peace talks. He knew Russian and the Russians very well, from his childhood in Petersburg, and he had recently taken part in the signing of the peace treaty at Brest-Litovsk. He was sent from Moscow to Petrograd as part of a commission aimed at improving the conditions of Austro-Hungarian prisoners of war. Contemporaries remembered him as a tall man with a bushy, reddish moustache. We don't know what made these two people of drastically different backgrounds and social environments, and of different citizenship, choose Petrograd as their residence, at a time when its population was on the brink of starvation, deserting, and gripped by typhus. They found themselves, of their own freewill, in the centre of a world catastrophe, at a time when others, who refused "to renounce the Old World", either fled or were killed. In 1918, Prince Leo Kotchoubey and Dolly's children left Petrograd for good, and reached Paris via the Ukraine. Their son Eugen Leonovich Prince Kotchoubey-Beauharnais (1894–1951) married Helen J. Pirce in Canada, had four daughters and died in Paris in 1951. His name is carved in Russian on a gravestone at the Saint-Genevieve-de Boise cemetery. Their offspring live in Europe and in the USA. Daria's daughter Princess Natalia Kotchoubey became a Catholic, and lived as a nun, Mother

Sophie, to become Mother Superior of a Dominican convent in Switzerland. Markezetti left a daughter by his first marriage in Vienna. The couple started a new life in the service of the Soviet government. Neither of them would see their children again.

In 1919, Maxim Gorky had established the *World Literature* publishing house in Petrograd, and on Markezetti's advice, premises were rented in a deserted mansion on Mokhovaya Street, at No.36. Over a period of four years the Publishers issued around two hundred books. A host of famous writers and scientists worked for the publishing house: A.Block, N.Gumilev, N.Marr, N.Krachkovsky, K.Chukovsky, and many more. However, publishing books wasn't the only aim of the organization. It was important not to allow those who had, not long ago, waited for, and so recently welcomed, the revolution, to starve or freeze to death without provisions or firewood, in the "cursed days" of the post-revolution (as writer Ivan Bunin put it) when they found themselves entirely unwanted. A photograph taken in 1919, celebrating the fiftieth birthday of Maxim Gorky, features the collective staff of the publishing house. The cause of the celebrations, Gorky, looks lost in thought, perhaps sensing the imminent and tragic fate that was being prepared for many of his colleagues. It is widely known that it was at this time that Gorky began to re-examine his relationship towards the Bolsheviks and their methods of leadership. The publishing house even attempted to provide for those who weren't working directly in it. The editor-in-chief's room was forever full of hungry individuals, waiting to pick up translations from foreign languages, and, as a rule, all of them belonged to the "former guard" who, like the writers, found themselves out, in the cold, after the revolution.

In the same publishing house, Markezetti organised, and was head of the Library of World Literature. He employed as his assistant Dora Leuchtenberg, who had previously worked as a clerk in the law department of the Petrograd

Theatre Association. A certain Mary Peterson describes the Dora Evgenievna of those days in her recollections, published as an article in the newspaper *The New Russian Word*, in the United States in 1964.[7]

She first met Dora at the palace of Count V.P. Zubov on Isaac's Square, which by then had been transformed into the State Institute for the History of Art, where hungry professors and their audiences had the chance of obtaining some much needed sustenance and provisions. On one particular day, instead of the usual apple jam, carrots and turnips, the Institute just cooked up millet soup, which was served to all from a bowl placed on a gorgeous antique table. A tall, stately lady in a dark and impeccable dress, with a ladle in her hand, was distributing the soup in the most elegant, unbelievably dignified manner. According to the author, everyone in Petrograd of the 1920s–30s knew this lady as the Duchess of Leuchtenberg, who, at her own risk, had created and granted herself that title. People were astonished that she managed to survive despite this reckless behaviour. "She claimed that in Switzerland she had known Lenin, or Trotsky, or both of them, and that the Smolny authorities had provided her with an immunity certificate," wrote Peterson.

In 1924, after Gorky's departure from Russia, *World Literature* merged with *Gosizdat*, the State Publishing House, and the library of foreign books, which was no longer needed, was administered as a department of the State Public Library. Both Dora Leuchtenberg and Victor Markezetti filled in forms in order to be enrolled on the library staff, giving information on themselves, however inaccurate or incomplete it may have been.

Dora Leuchtenberg and Peterson became working colleagues, and the former was remembered as a striking and extraordinary figure, verging on a living monument from a different era. "The lady advanced in a stately manner, stopped in front of the tables, stretching out her hand favourably, as if to be kissed (though nobody kissed it), and I was amazed by the fact that many of the staff immediately found a pretext to end their conversations and disappear, whilst others, having caught sight of her, tried to hide behind bookcases or columns...I did the same myself...She couldn't have worked as a provocateur or a secret informant, as the more cowardly asserted, but her speech, in all five languages, was studded with glimmering diamonds in bejewelled settings, such as the name of her grandmother, Maria Nikolaevna, grandfather Maximilian Duke of Leuchtenberg, uncle Grand Duke this-and-that, and even (worst of all!) Uncle Max of Baden! (in 1918, Chancellor of Germany – Z.B.). All that annoyed and excited the fantasies of the real informant who were hiding themselves behind the bookcases." Anecdotes about Dora were often recounted, though the young co-workers felt no animosity towards her at all. They liked to chat and laugh, retelling funny and occasionally tragic episodes of Dora's past and present life. The last of such anecdotes, both comic and tragic, and dating from 1931/32, was recounted thus:

Dora, anxiously: What am I to do with my grandfather? He was buried at the St John of Jerusalem Maltese Chapel, on the grounds of the Corps of Pages... which is now used as a Soviet military school...Now "they" want to put a 'Red corner' in the chapel, and have asked me to take my grandfather out. Good Lord! Such a magnificent building! Rosewood doors from Malmaison!

Questioner: Did you try to petition the Commission for the Protection of Art and History for help?

Dora: They say, they can't help...you see, he was the Grand Master of the Maltese Order! I have no right to touch his relics without permission from the present Grand Master!

Questioner: Do they still exist?

Dora: Of course! In Bavaria! I'm not allowed to write abroad without KGB permission, and the KGB might not permit it. Or the Grand Master may be against...

Dora decided that it was better to transfer the relics by herself, before her grandfather could be thrown out of his grave. "I'll just hire a horse and take him to the Smolensky cemetery" was her reasonable decision. We can only guess at how the Duchess's problem was eventually resolved. However, today there is no tomb, lovingly designed at the behest of the widowed Grand Duchess Maria, to be found at the St. John of Jerusalem Chapel. The tomb was reported as having been designed as an altar with a sarcophagus, and the answer to the mystery of its disappearance is no doubt to be found in the repeated desecration, and virtual destruction, of the church itself*.

Throughout her career as librarion Dora only went abroad once. In 1924, she visited Finland for two months where she stayed at General Gustav Mannerheim's as a guest, her first husband having been a good friend of the general. She may have visited the grave of her husband Grävenitz, and in addition, many of Grävenitz's relations lived in Finland after their escape from Petrograd in 1917–18. Their present descendants claim that many of their family walked across the ice of the Gulf of Finland in order to reach safety.

Her visit to Finland, however, may have had another purpose.

From an archival report in criminal case No.36433, investigating Zakhar Alexandrovich Sharin-Chernov, born 1894, who came to the USSR from abroad:

"In November 1924, a certain Zakhar Alexandrovich Sharin-Chernov, a former colonel, was arrested whilst crossing the Finno-Russian border. During his arrest he was injured, and as a result he was moved to the hospital of the German Red Cross in Leningrad. During questioning he stated that he had journeyed to the USSR on a mission from the monarchical group of Grand Duke Nicholas Nikolaevich, in order to establish contacts with the military leadership circles of the RKKA (the Red Army – Z.B.). He was to become a legal citizen in the

---

* The Chapel has been recently rebuilt.

USSR, in Leningrad, and to meet couriers arriving from abroad, and spread illegal literature. Sharin-Chernov's main mission was to organize insurgent detachments and terrorist groups, and to carry out terrorist acts.

"He also stated that before being sent to the USSR, members of the Finnish secret service gave him a password and a secret signal for a rendezvous in Leningrad at No.36 Mokhovaya Street, with the Duchess of Leuchtenberg and her husband Markezetti. Whilst receiving treatment at the prison hospital, with the knowledge of, and on the orders of OGPU, he made contact with Leuchtenberg, who then, with her husband Markezetti, visited him in hospital. Leuchtenberg and Markezetti sent Sharin-Chernov's letters abroad and brought him letters that had arrived from abroad for him…"[8]

At that time the counterespionage department of the Soviet secret police, with the help of their *agents provocateur* from *Trest* organization, convinced the leaders of the Russian émigré community in France to send their own agents to sound out the situation in Russia, to explore the social tensions, to assess the problems with the army and police, and the general mood. Two prominent leaders of the monarchist movement were Grand Duke Nicholas Nikolaevich (Nikolasha) and General Alexander Kutepov. Soviet intelligence officers tried to involve them both into their fake conspiracy. The shocking truth about *Trest* and its provocation work finally emerged only in 1927. In all likelihood Dora could be weaved into such a conspiracy, with her growing hatred toward the Bolsheviks.*

At the beginning of 1926, the OGPU [once CheKa] board sentenced Sharin-Chernov to be shot. Dora and Victor were not touched.

In 1927, Dora Leuchtenberg became a Soviet citizen and received an identification card of the USSR. Markezetti remained an Austrian citizen right up until his arrest in 1937. How

---

* The descendants of Nicholas Nikolaevich, Jr., categorically deny any involvement on the part of the sick Grand Duke in political intrigues during his final years. – Z.B.

should one regard the final words of M.Peterson's article: "Dora's collaboration with Soviet power was paid for in a labour camp?" Following their arrest, it was whispered that they had both been exiled to the town of Kem. Perhaps they attempted to recruit her, through fear, threats and blackmail, or through exploiting her patriotic feelings. The reality, for the time being, is not known. The list of agents in the secret service is protected by a 75-year period of secrecy, and that 75 years has yet to elapse. Yet some recent scant and partly inaccurate data suggest that both Victor and Dora happened to somehow collaborate with the Soviet securities. Although motifs and details remain unresolved.

We can glean some clues as to the atmosphere in which they lived during those years, by studying their personal files. In the autumn of 1929, a special commission of the Public Library was summoned to check the work of the former foreign books department of *World Literature*, which was now part of the Public Library. An article published in the *Red Newspaper* under the title "Great-granddaughter of Nikolai Palkin"* was the pretext for the investigation. The article had it that there was a good deal of malpractice being carried out by the department head Markezetti, and by his wife. It was claimed that their luxuriously furnished apartment was too large for two persons, that they had not increased their maid's wage, that they used firewood from the library to heat their own apartment, and that they subscribed to French fashion magazines at the library's expense. In addition Dora was accused of anti-Semitism. The article itself was anonymously written, and the author was not found.

The commission worked until November, and Dora was invited to attend one of their meetings in person. The matter discussed was her relationship with her co-workers. They complained that Dora intimidated them by mentioning her

* Nikolai Palkin ('Iron Rod') was a derogatory name of Emperor Nicholas I much approved by the Bolsheviks.

connections with OGPU, and even with the Central Committee, as she alleged that formerly she had been acquainted with Lenin and that Gorky himself had recommended her for work in the Public Library. Dora rejected the idea of any acquaintance with Lenin, but acknowledged her OGPU contacts, claiming that many former Imperial Army officers now served in that organisation. Though the commission failed to prove the majority of the accusations, it did come to the conclusion that Dora's work in the library was no longer necessary or, indeed, advisable.

From the protocol of that meeting: "…in spite of the fact that, from the October revolution to the present, D.E.Leuchtenberg has lived and worked in Soviet Russia, she has failed to free herself of the prejudices of her class, and this can be seen in her attitude toward co-workers, and in the evidence of anti-Semitism and haughtiness."

Dora was left without work, and only returned to the library in 1931. A document has survived, which notes her enrolment as an assistant on the staff of a special archive at the Public Library. In the same year, they were deprived of some of their living space in the apartment at No.36 Mokhovaya, and were left with only two rooms. There is another document from that time, which gives Markezetti the right to extra living space, and indicates his monthly salary as being 140 roubles.

The final document in the personal file of our subject comes from August 1937. It is an order for Dora to be sacked from the library. The document testifies to criminal negligence and a lack of responsibility in the storing secret papers, which was incompatible with her work at the library's special archive. The report from the head of the special archive, V.A.Shalov by name, notes that Leuchtenberg, D.E. "stubbornly ignored instructions, for example: gave out books without the required documentation, made translations for unknown purposes and for unknown persons from forbidden journals, allowed a mass of forbidden and explicitly counter-revolutionary literature to be distributed in the reading room, etc.". Soon after, Markezetti was also fired.

There are more records, but from a different source. Archival file No.11437, from the archives of the UKGB LO*, charging Leuchtenberg D.E.:

Certificate

The 3rd department of the UKGB LO verifies that citizen Leuchtenberg Dora Evgenievna, born - 1881, in Munich, a German by birth, citizen of the USSR, employee of the Public Library, resident at 36 Mokhovaya St., apt.3, hiding her social background, married to Markezetti V.A. - a citizen of Austria, and a verified Austrian intelligence officer, - is acting as an intelligence agent of the Austrian Military Headquarters, and is implementing their orders on the territory of the USSR. Leuchtenberg Dora Evgenievna is to be arrested and charged under art.58-1a UK RSFSR. September 9, 1937.

Three days before, on the 6th of September, the UNKVD LO received a cable from Moscow: "Arrest Markezetti, Victor Alexandrovich, citizen of Austria. Agreed NKID Potyomkin. Minaev. 6/9-37. 07:37." (i.e.Ministry of Foreign Affairs).

They were both arrested on the 10th of September 1937. The search protocol noted as having been confiscated: a sword and scabbard, a silver cigarette case (by the way with an inscription in Russian "for intelligence service"), 12 items of various foreign orders. Correspondence bearing no relation to the case was destroyed. They were allowed to take a minimum of personal things with them, after which the rooms were sealed. Later on it became known that before 1937, and on agreement with Moscow, Markezetti was connected with Major-General M.Ronghe, Head of the Austrian intelligence, who was arrested by the Gestapo in 1938. In 1975, a retired

---

* Archive of the UKGB LO – the Managing Committee for State Security for the Leningrad Oblast (Region).

major of UNKVD LO Ya.O.Khaskin, who once worked at the special archive of the Public Library, also reported about Markezetti's contacts with the NKVD in those days.

Interrogations lasted throughout October. Needless to say, they were found guilty on all counts, and each page of the interrogation papers was individually signed. Yet, during the course of the questioning the lady's signature drastically changed, and the final papers were signed by a 67-year-old (sic!), tired and broken woman. Dora Evgenievna signed all the documents admitting that she was the wife of Markezetti, an arrested member of the Gestapo; that she was connected with an intelligence-terrorist group of German political emigrants in Leningrad, created by agents of the Gestapo; that she was aware of the preparation of a terrorist act on the life of A.A.Zhdanov, the famed Communist party boss; that in Finland in 1924, she had been recruited by a monarchist-terrorist organization; that her apartment was a location for secret meetings, and that during the period from 1924 to 1928 the apartment was visited by six agents from foreign counter-revolutionary organizations.

On October the 29th, an Extraordinary NKVD Meeting sentenced D.E.Leuchtenberg to be shot along with a "resident of the German intelligence" M.M.Dobranitsky, the former Director of the Public Library.

Report

On November 5th, 1937, the sentence on Leuchtenberg Dora Evgenievna, in accordance with the order of GB Commissar Zakovonny A.P., the Head of UNKVD LO, dated November 4,1937, of No.191222, as well as the NARKOM VNUDEL order, dated November 2nd, 1937, of No.113096, was executed personally by the Commandant of UNKVD LO, Senior Lieutenant Polikarpov A.P. The above-mentioned condemned person has been shot.

Commandant UNKVD LO
Senior Lieutenant of GB   Polikarpov.

Victor Markezetti was interrogated and tormented much longer, right through December, until he was forced to confess that he had been an agent of the German intelligence services from 1935 onwards, and that he led a militant terrorist group, received arms from the German Consul in Leningrad for the carrying out of terrorist acts, and that under his leader-ship seven bombs had been prepared for the attempt on Comrade Zhdanov's life. It was in the same December 1937, until which time he had remained a citizen of Austria with permission to reside in the USSR, that he became a Soviet citizen in a cell for tortures. Now it became possible to execute him.

Classified

Act

On January 15th, 1937, I, Commandant UNKVD LO Senior Lieutenant of State Security, Polikarpov A.P. in accordance with the order of the Deputy Head of the UNKVD LO – Major of State Security, Comrade Garin, of the 14th of January 1938, of No. 219058, as well as the NARKOM VNUDEL order, dated January 12th, 1938, of No.450242, executed the sentence in relation to MARKEZETTI VICTOR ALEXANDROVICH.

The above-mentioned condemned person WAS SHOT.

Commandant UNKVD LO Senior Lieutenant of State Security   (Polikarpov)
                                     signature
                                     15th of January 1938

However, the tragic history of both condemned prisoners is not complete. In June 1975, a Military Tribunal of the Leningrad Military District overturned the ruling of the Commission of the NKVD of the 10th of January 1938, in relation to MARKEZETTI, Victor Alexandrovich, and the case was thrown out "for lack of an offence". On the same day it was established that the executed Markezetti V.A. had been arrested despite a total lack of evidence, that his confessions during interrogation could in no way be corroborated by any objective evidence, and that "former staffers of the UNKVD LO (three surnames) who took part in the investigation of the Markezetti case, had permitted serious violations against the principles of socialist legislature to take place in their work, including the falsification of criminal proceedings."[10]

Dora Leuchtenberg ceased to be listed as "enemy of people" since 11 May 1989, in accordance with the decision of LVO Military Procurator.

Epilogue

The house at 36 Mokhovaya Street has survived. It is now a music school. Classrooms are housed in what was formerly apartment No.3. One of the rooms contains a grand piano which, as they say, has stood there since time immemorial. If we are to judge by the date on it, 1901, and the label which reads "Inventory. Petrograd. 1920", it could tell a tale or two. It was from this room that Dora and Victor were taken away forever.

Looking at the portraits in the Hermitage, it's hard to believe that such a harsh fate befell a woman whose veins coursed with the blood of Catherine the Great and Joséphine Beauharnais.

The stakes for her 'kidding with Soviet power' were too high. Long, long ago her great-great-grandfather, Viscount Alexander de Beauharnais had chosen the way to collaborate with the revolutionary French powers. His correspondence with members of the Convent was kept at the Mariinsky Palace by his grandson Maximilian. Viscount Alexander Beauharnais had ended his life on a guillotine, as well as his offspring Countess Daria Beauharnais of Russia was shot in the back of her head in other time, by other revolutionary power. At present Dolly's descendants have no idea when and how she ended her life.

REFERENCES

1 Belyakova, p.209–211

2 Archive of RNL,
    dated July 1925

3 Mossolov, p.130

4 A.M., p.126

5 Nicholas II, *Vospominaniia,
    dnevniki*, p.292

6 RGIA, *opis'* 17, *delo* 537

7 B.W., p.296

8 March, 1964

9 Archive FCB (NKVD LO),
    delo 1433

10 Archive
    FCB, *delo* 27-H-75

All Fell in Love with Ella

*Among my Russian relatives
I like Ella most of all.*

From a conversation between
His Royal Highness Charles,
the Prince of Wales,
and the author

Grand Duchess Elizabeth Feodorovna of Russia, who is better remembered as Ella, and under her maiden name as a Hessian princess, occupies a place of her own amongst the members of the Romanov dynasty. Moreover, among the grand duchesses of the late 19th–early 20th century she was virtually unequalled as an arresting personality bereft of ambition and egoism, harmonious and noble both in her aspirations and in her actions. Most notably, in her final hours, she performed an astonishing moral feat. She epitomised Anton Chekhov's dream of an individual who is 'all perfect in character, soul, clothes, and thoughts'. Grand Duke Alexander Mikhailovich of Russia wrote about her: "No nobler woman has left the imprint of her personality on the bloodstained pages of Russian history."[1]

Many facets of Grand Duchess Elizabeth's nature can be explained by the events of her early childhood, her upbringing, family traditions and influences, as well as by the circumstances of her life in St. Petersburg. However, her new Russian sensations, experiences and surroundings were not given a sufficient research.

Elizabeth was born on November 1, 1864, in a small town of Darmstadt, the capital of a small grand duchy of Hesse, cut in half by the Rhine River. Formerly known as Hesse-Darmstadt, it occupied, alongside five other medium-sized grand duchies, an intermediate position, both in terms of territory and political importance, among the other German states which ranged from four larger kingdoms, led by powerful Prussia, through four duchies* to numerous pocket-principalities.

The Hessian House was regarded as one of the most ancient dynasties in Europe. Its founder Giselbert in the 9th century had also ruled Lotharingia-Brabant. The Hesse family counted among their ancestors the legendary St. Elizabeth of Thuringia, or Hungary (1207–1231), a daughter of a Hungarian king, who had been canonized by the Catholic Church for her charitable life, which had been lived in poverty. She built hospitals in Marburg, spent enormous money on the poor, and, in the end, sold all her jewels and dresses so that she could give help to those in need. After the death of her husband, Landgrave Ludwig IV of Thuringia, she had joined the Franciscan Third Order and took care of lepers. It was in honour of this Catholic saint that Elizabeth was given her name, but she was baptized into the Lutheran church and then brought up in a distinctly Anglican Christian culture. At baptism, the parents could have no idea of how closely their infant girl was to follow the fate of her saintly ancestress.

In the palace, topped with the red-and-white Hessian flag, many royal betrothals and marriages were celebrated, strengthening the long-lasting blood ties of the Hessian rulers with other German Houses, and with the sovereigns of Mantua, Parma, Poland, Sweden and Sicily. Even today Hessian blood runs in the veins of the British, Prussian, Russian, Swedish, Danish and Greek royal families.

Family relations between the Darmstadt dukes and the House of Romanov were old and strong. Princess Wilhelmina Louise (rechristened Natalia Alexeyevna) happened to be the first wife of the then Grand Duke and future Emperor Paul I. The young Hesse-Darmstadt Princess Maximiliana Wilhelmina Sophia Marie was chosen as bride by the heir apparent to the

* After Prussia (1701), Saxony, Württemberg and Bavaria became likewise kingdoms; the grand duchies of Baden, Oldenburg, Mecklenburg-Schwerin, Mecklenburg-Strelitz and Saxe-Weimar-Eisenach; duchies such as Saxe-Altenburg, Saxe-Coburg and Gotha, Saxe-Meiningen and Anhalt.

Russian throne, Grand Duke Alexander who, in 1839, had been travelling in Europe. She became the Russian Empress Marie Alexandrovna (1824–1880), and was both Ella's great-aunt and mother-in-law, though due to the Empress's premature death she never gave Ella her blessing as a daughter-in-law. A distant cousin of the reigning Grand Duke of Hesse at that time was Marie Feodorovna, the consort of Emperor Alexander III.

In the middle of the last century, Grand Duke Ludwig III stood at the head of the Hessian family. His younger brother Charles (Karl) was expected to be his successor. The English Queen Victoria (1819–1901) chose Karl's eldest handsome and affable son Ludwig as husband for her second daughter Alice. Yet, their wedding was delayed because of the sudden death of Prince Consort Albert in December of 1861. The Queen was widowed whilst approaching forty-two years of age. She was deeply affected by the death of her dearly beloved husband, and all her strength was sapped by grief. For days on, she lay motionless on her bed, rising only to make frequent visits to a room, where the body of Prince Albert lay in state. The eighteen-year-old Princess Alice had to organize the funeral. Through her devoted attention and care Victoria finally recovered from her despair. In later years Queen Victoria lavishly embellished London with statues and monuments to her late husband and the grandfather of Ella.

The wedding of Alice and Ludwig took place in the summer of 1862, in strict keeping with Albert's wishes. He had blessed the match, planned the ceremony and ordered the bride's robe to make it a joyous celebration. Instead it took place with as little ceremony as possible, at the seaside gloomy mansion of Osborne on the Isle of Wight. Victoria was still in mourning, and Alice was dressed in a trousseau, partly of black. The guests who were dressed in half-mourning soon departed from such a sad wedding.

Life in Darmstadt, the capital of Hesse, proved much more dull and trivial than the young duchess could have expected. A decade of continual political disagreement ensued, growing into conflicts and wars. Ella's childhood was by no means serene, and with some justification she could be dubbed "a war child".

In the loosely federated German lands, the political situation was aggravated by the aspirations of Prussia and her Hohenzollern rulers towards domination. The chance for supremacy soon came true with the appointment of Count Otto von Bismarck, an unscrupulous wily diplomat, as its chancellor. Indeed Bismarck had achieved the virtually impossible through the unification of many separate duchies into one state under Prussia's aegis. Finally he accomplished the dream of which he had spoken in St. Petersburg salons long before, in the early era of Emperor Alexander II, by ordering the Prussian army to march into those states which were still claiming independence. Thus, Hanover, Saxony, and Nassau were occupied.

In 1866, Hesse sided with Austria in an unfortunate war against Prussia. In 1870, another war was declared, and the Prussian army crossed the Hessian border. Alice had seen her husband off to the battlefields as Ludwig took command of the national cavalry. Little Ella and her sister Victoria, together with the Duchess who assisted in the military hospitals, helped the wounded and visited widows and orphans. The war gave her harsh lessons in compassion, mercy and the giving of aid to people in distress. Ella grew up with a pronounced sensitivity to the sufferings of others.

Over a period of seven weeks the Prussian army devastated Darmstadt and ruined Ludwig's property. In 1871, Hesse was forcibly included into the newly created German Empire. Bismarck's triumph came on January 18, 1871, when he organized solemn proclamation of his sovereign as Kaiser Wilhelm I, or Emperor of Germany, in Versailles, in the Hall of Mirrors.

The loss of independence meant impoverishment for the duchy. The House of Hesse had never been wealthy, but under the post-war conditions, the country and the duke's family paid reparations in addition to losing many of their most profitable lands. It was necessary to make economies in order to build a new residence. Alice had to dismiss several servants and drastically reduce the number of receptions and theatre visits. Every effort was made to comply with the shrinking annual budget. The detailed accounting became so complex and strained that Alice had to beg the Queen to pay her hotel bills during her rare trips. In the end, tired of begging, Alice learnt to travel unattended, and stayed in cheap hotels.

War and financial hardships took their toll on the marital relationship, already strained by the dissimilar natures of the couple. Alice was earnest, sensitive, pious, and sophisticated, Ludwig was a bluff, unintellectual and good-natured soldier, a fan of the outdoors, sherry and horses ("a pretty simple person", *chelovek nemudrenyi*, in the opinion of Petersburgers).[2] Nonetheless they were devoted to each other.

What love there had been vanished along with the illusions, and only bitterness persisted. Apart from the disappointments of her family life, Alice remained deeply hurt by the feeling of a foreigner who did not fit into the clan of Darmstadt connections and society. Grievances badly affected her mood and health. Melancholy and nervous anxiety marked her character, as did evident exhaustion. Her health also suffered as a result of numerous pregnancies. In the first twelve years of her married life Alice gave birth to seven children. In 1863, her eldest daughter Victoria (1863–1950) was born, later marrying her cousin Prince Louis of Battenberg (1854–1921). Then followed Elizabeth (1864 –1918), Irene (1866–1953), the future wife of Prince Henry of Prussia, and cousin of Kaiser Wilhelm II. Thereafter appeared Ernest Ludwig (Ernie, 1868–1937) and Friedrich William (Frittie, 1870–1873). Her sixth child Alix (1872–1918), who subsequently became the last Russian Empress, was given a lengthy string of names at baptism: Her Royal Highness Princess Alix Victoria Helena Louise Beatrice of Hesse-and-by-Rhine. Their last daughter Marie (May, 1874–78) did not live long. Nannies were too expensive, and Alice nursed and looked after the children herself, although aided by a pitifully low number of servants.

Princess Alice gave herself wholeheartedly to the up-bringing and education of their children, inspiring them with a love of God and the rule of law, hoping that they would grow up as honourable citizens, noble, unselfish, and responsive to kind deeds. They were taught that one's sense of responsibility should always dwarf one's personal needs. Indeed, in Darm-stadt, the children were raised in a manner unlike that preva-lent in other royal families, where the reigning parents gave preference to state and social obligations. From early childhood the Hessian princesses learned how to make beds, to clean the nursery with broom and duster, to heat a fireplace and bake an apple pie. They lived in, and enjoyed, a world of genuine and simple pleasures.

The irreproachable nanny Mrs. Orchard ('Orchie' later accompanied Alix to Russia) ruled the nursery firmly, in accor-dance with Princess Alice's instructions. The children had to get up early, as the lessons began promptly at seven in the morning. A simple breakfast was served at nine o'clock. Dur-ing the day there would be unpretentious food: meat, rice, baked potatoes and apples. Daily care and kindness towards the household pets was encouraged; the children looked after a pet fox, a wild boar, bunnies, pet sheep, and a Shetland pony.

In her early years, Ella did not provide any surprise, or demonstrate any spectacular promise. She grew up as a normal child, fairly healthy and naughty, and studied without any particular brilliance or enthusiasm, but was the prettiest of the siblings. She loved nature, music, and drew well, as her sense of line and colour developed at an early stage. Daily life in the palace was organized along English lines and traditions, which blended well with the German love of order and practi-cality, and the virtue of sufficing with the simple and eternal. Their masters were German, but all the children spoke both English and German fluently.

From childhood, fortune showed little for Ella. Its first horrid blow was the death of the two-year-old Frittie, who suffered in-curably from haemophilia (until recently it was believed that this terrible ailment and gene was transmitted from Queen Victoria to male offspring). Sitting in a drawing room, Alice saw Frittie fall from an open bow window onto the stone terrace a few feet below, and although it was believed that he only suffered a minor injury, the boy died from internal brain haemorrhaging by nightfall. From that day on, a presentiment of inevitable grief and peril pursued the mother and was in turn transferred to the children. The girls developed a strong belief in the judgement of God, in the inevitability of fate, and in preparation for eternity. They became fervent and exalted Christians.

In 1877, Ella's father became Grand Duke Ludwig IV of Hesse. The duties of the First Lady of the court and land took away the last of Alice's health resources. More often than not her daughters would find her seeking refuge, lying on her sofa, and she would frequently speak to them of death and reunion in Heaven. Thus the seeds of fatalism were sown, as well as foreboding of the approaching perils and troubles. A resignation to future sufferings was deeply ingrained. Later on, far from home, in their new Russian surroundings, these foreboding and sensations would bring fruit and affect the souls and deeds of both Hessian princesses.

In 1878, almost every member of the family contracted diphtheria, and for little May it proved fatal. Worn out by the punishing effort of nursing her family, Alice fell ill herself. During delirious spells of fever Alice had visions of her father, Frittie and May, all calling her to Heaven. After being ill a few days, Alice died in December 1878, at the age of thirty-five. On the same day the childhood of her offspring drew to a close.

Queen Victoria promised to act as second mother to her motherless grandchildren. Ella and her sisters spent a significant part of their youth in England under the tutelage of their grandmother, who instructed them in the arts of being an accomplished, dutiful princess, endowing them with dignity and responsibility. Victoria taught etiquette to her granddaughters, the skill of negotiating one's way round a room with stately grace, of seating oneself properly whilst in courtly dress, of carrying out the social duties required of a person of royal blood. She closely supervised the girls' schooling, and encouraged progress in their education, advising them as to what to read, and which sciences and music to study.

Legend has it that once, when the four young sisters went for a walk in Richmond Park outside of London, they met an old gypsy woman who wanted to read their palms. She predicted happiness for Victoria and Irene, but grew troubled at once when examining the palms of Ella and Alix. She predicted that they would marry in a distant country and both would be unhappy.

England became Ella's second home. On her mother's British side alone she had 28 relatives, whom Grand Duke Ludwig termed "the royal mob". Osborne, Windsor, Frogmore and Balmoral in Scotland were favourite residences of carefree youth. In Darmstadt, Ella was much more concerned about her father and the younger children, whom she had to comfort, and whose tears she had to wipe. Another "royal mob" was made up of her German relations on the continent.

Their Prussian cousin Wilhelm, who at that stage was in his late teens, frequently visited the Hessian children. At the age of 26, he became Kaiser of Germany. Willy was an insecure, restless man, with an enormous sense of his physical inadequacy. The boy had been born with a deformed arm*, and as a guest, he behaved rudely and selfishly. He would demand that everybody ride or shoot, or play tennis. Frequently he would throw down his racket in the middle of game and insist that everyone go rowing or bicycling. When Willy got tired or bored, he ordered that the younger cousins sit round him, and he would read aloud to them from the Bible. Wilhelm had become convinced that God had personally chosen him for the German throne, reasoning that he possessed some special qualities. As the future German emperor he appointed himself leader among the young people.

Cousin Willy was madly in love with Ella, her beauty entranced him. He was nineteen and a student at Bonn Universi-

---

* Due to a defective left arm, "the Kaiser at meals could not cut a piece of meat without help," asserts R. Massie.

ty, but instead of studying he wrote love poems. Willy shadowed Ella everywhere, sat opposite, gazed and devoured her with his eyes, when she spoke. He frightened Ella who was only fourteen, and his presence in itself was appalling. But her good upbringing and natural kindness prevented the princess from being outwardly rude, and from even commenting on his unnecessary and unwanted attentions.

His efforts were in vain. He had little attraction for her, and the idea of being German empress had little appeal. The militarism and cold formality of the Berlin court had repelled the Hessians. Besides, the sad and lonely life of Ella's aunt Vicky led as crown princess, who was treated with hostility at the Prussian court because she was English, served as a warning to her.

Ella made her own choice. She married Grand Duke Sergei (1857–1905) of Russia whom Willy tried to blacken in her eyes by any means possible. Thereafter he refused to talk to her in private, and only during official receptions used to utter two or three polite words. His passion did not die with passing time. It is no accident that the German ambassador to Sweden, through an intermediary person, offered Elizabeth a chance to leave Russia during WW I, when spontaneous persecution of people of German origin began in Russia.

At sixteen, Ella began to "come out", and at her first ball she enchanted a number of admirers of both sex, and some were even smitten with love for her. At twenty, she blossomed fantastically: tall and slender, with golden hair and grey-blue eyes, one of which was dotted with a spot of brown, giving her glance a most unusual effect. Her kindness and friendliness were in keeping with her attractive appearance. The Queen wrote to Lord Wolseley on May 16th, 1884: "...she is a real beauty and none of your made up beauties of English society, but so fresh and blooming." The prospect of her favourite granddaughter's marriage filled the Queen with dread. The day after Ella's departure for Russia, Victoria wept over the match and with sorrow predicted that she would never again see Ella as happy as she was the last 5 years.

Ella knew Sergei from her nursery days. They frequently met in Heiligenberg, at Prince Alexander's of Hesse*, the favourite brother of Russian Empress Maria Alexandrovna, who had morganatically married a Russian lady-in-waiting, Julia v. Hauke. Marie, as German relatives named her, often took her youngest sons, Sergei and Paul, with her. The boys differed so greatly! In Paul's room, wooden horses 'were in pasture' everywhere, and other toys abounded. Yet, even in early childhood, Sergei preferred an abundance of icons and holy images of various sizes, which made for quite a sight in a nursery. Could it have been the result of two winters spent in Moscow, at the Neskuchny Palace, due to his poor health? Could it have been the influence of Metropolitan Philaret and the liturgies at Chudov Monastery? Of all his lessons, Sergei preferred history, and as a child he passionately loved Moscow, the ancient Russian capital, and the Russia of a bygone age.

It's quite probable that little Ella was secretly in love with her Russian uncle**, who was 8 years her senior, and seemed serious, clever, extremely elegant and handsome, due to his particular highbred beauty. Her girlish affection later developed into a more profound feeling. Of all his brothers, Sergei, the fifth son of Alexander II, was 'born in the purple'***, and he reminded Ella of his mother Empress Marie whom the Hessians had always adored and considered a veritable saint. He was good looking, tall and slim, standing erect in his characteristic posture, with head up and chest out. He had blond thick crewcut hair, small but fine facial features, light-blue eyes, a fine

* Alexander (1823–88), the fifth child in the family of Grand Duke Ludwig II of Hesse, Marie (1824–80) was the last sixth child. Prince Alexander married Julia von Hauke, a lady-in-waiting to Empress Alexandra Feodorovna and the daughter of a Russian general-in-artillery. Duke Ludwig III created her Countess, and in 1858 – Princess of Battenberg.

** Sergei is often called Ella's cousin instead of her uncle by mistake: Duke Karl of Hesse, Ella's grandfather, and Empress Marie were brother and sister.

*** Sergei, as well as Paul, was born when his father had already become Emperor.

moustache, which he later exchanged for a closely trimmed beard. In stark contrast to his brothers, Sergei was indifferent to beauties, did not hunt animals on principle, and openly disliked Germany, Prussia in particular, preferring England and France. German princesses seemed boring to him, "except one", he used to say, and everyone knew whom he meant.

Indeed, Elizabeth could never fit into the mould of a typical German princess. Wars, bereavement, nursing, an austere upbringing and her mother's religious anxiety had given her an adult's outlook while still a girl. In talks and books she searched for truth and spiritual certainties. She regarded marriage being more than wifely submissiveness, motherly devotion, and rigid procreation of a husband's dynasty. She awaited an intellectual, sensitive man, to avoid her mother's fate in a marriage mental isolation.

In September 1879, Grand Duke Ludwig's aunt, the ailing Empress Marie of Russia came to rest at Heiligenberg. Her sons Sergei and Paul now grown men arrived a few days later. There was no evidence of a romance. Yet, in a matter of a few months Ella's sympathy and compassion grew immensely upon learning that Sergei lost both his beloved parents. Empress Marie, whose health continued to deteriorate until she was little more than an emaciated skeleton, died on June 2nd, 1880. No one was present at her bedside. Her husband stayed in Tsarskoe Selo, along with his mistress and their three illegitimate children. For hours, the dead Empress remained alone in her locked bedroom, while the elder grand dukes and other inhabitants of the Winter Palace crowded in the next room. The sorrowful and confused assemblage was waiting for the Emperor to come from his summer residence and enter the bedroom first. He finally arrived by 10 a.m. That blow fell heavily on the younger children who adored their mother and treated her with the utmost tenderness and devotion. Yet, the drama was not over.

Alexander waited only the minimum forty days required by church law to marry Princess Catherine Dolgoruky. It was the first time a Russian ruler married a Russian since Peter the

Great. What a slap in the face of all relations! The marriage was morganatic, but their three children were legitimized. Catherine was reportedly determined to be crowned empress. At the time, the youngest sons remained in Italy for medical cure, and that shocking scandalous news made them cry, and caused profound depression in such a religious person as Sergei. Their sister Marie wrote to Alexander II: "I pray that myself and my junior brothers, who were particularly close to Mama, would one day be able to forgive you."[3] The news of a horrific accident in St. Petersburg followed next.

On March 1, 1881, Alexander II, the most liberal of the 19th century tsars, was murdered by nihilist-terrorists. He implemented the liberation of the serfs and ventured Russia on the way to modernization. His era witnessed trial by jury, creation of limited local self-government (*zemstvo*), freer press, women higher education, etc. The very morning of assassination, the Emperor had signed a constitutional manifesto to improve Russia's governance, which was found on his desk unattended. The Romanovs reckoned that his cruel murder was not a coincidence or irony, but a sign that Russia's course was wrong. His eldest son became Tsar Alexander III, inflexibly determined to yield nothing in liberal concessions. Instead, the new Emperor, a nationalist-conservative, embarked on a policy of repression and reaction in defence of his absolute power.

The effect on Sergei was even graver. He hardly made his way from Florence to St. Petersburg to take part in the funeral ceremony. The foundations of his life were blown up. Henceforth, an intense hatred for any liberalism turned him into a strict reactionary, determined to defend autocracy by all means. He took over the command of the Preobrazhensky Guards regiment from his brother Alexander. The guards, a closed male fraternity, were noted for pederasty and heavy drinking. It is quite probable that emotionally devastated Sergei was involved in such a companionship with its peculiar vices.

In the fatal year 1881, when Sergei and Paul became orphans, they decided to visit the Holy Land in the company of their cousin Constantine. The latter served as a lieutenant on the *Duke of Edinburgh* warship which was navigating in the Mediterranean Sea. They called at the ports of Egypt, Algeria, Greece, and Palestine. That journey made a particular strong impact on Sergei, who much assisted the Russian pilgrims along the way. He also donated large sums of money for the excavation work carried out in Jerusalem. Upon return he became set on marrying Ella. He perhaps needed a substitute for his parents, or an ideal of purity more than he felt any passion for her. The fear of nihilism made him hurry in his courting. Late in 1882, with Paul, he arrived in Hesse.

Ella, knowing little of her uncle's private life, was profoundly moved with his drama. Her sympathy was strongly aroused to this cultured, sensitive, *distingue*, suffering man, who loved Italian art which was also her favourite. His increased theological knowledge and his deeply ingrained religious fervour had a particular appeal to Ella. She fancied a noble, deeply pious soul beneath his haughty front, and hoped that she might soften and soothe him. At eighteen, when deciding about love and marriage, she had no idea of how hollow such a marriage would be.

Petersburg high society dubbed Sergei a "mock saint" (*sviatosha*). The *beau monde* regarded him cold and inflexible, and not without reason. In his faith he was entirely under the influence of Pobedonostsev*, his tutor and guardian in religious matters. Sergei was not a sociable, charming man, and he usually seemed withdrawn, his face expressing sadness or cold alienation. Among his relations he preferred Paul and cousin Constantine. The elite of Petersburg had noticed the high value he attached to religion after the trip to Jerusalem. Here is an impression of Count Lamsdorf, a high state functionary in St. Petersburg: "…had dinner at Grand Duke Sergei's. His Highness might be capable of something, for he is interested in serious matters, and not just the routine *poshol* [go out!]

* K.P.Pobedonostsev, the Ober-procurator of the Holy Synod, was a conservative traditionalist who regarded the parliamentary system as "the worst lie of the century".

of the other grand dukes. The Grand Duke is an embodiment of tactfulness, discretion and endurance after returning from Jerusalem."[4]

However, the engagement did not proceed smoothly. The Romanovs appeared alien to Queen Victoria, who had had deep misgivings about the family, though only two Russian sovereigns had caused her trouble. Nicholas I had been a notable adversary during the Crimean War (1853–55), as was his son, Emperor Alexander II, during the Russo-Turkish campaign (1877–78). Russia's military success and the threat of her growing influence in the Balkans deepened a form of russophobia in England. During the period of Sergei's courtship, in London, the anglophobia of Emperor Alexander III was likewise taken into account. Victoria loathed Russia for good reasons and her profound distrust was not easily appeased. The Queen's words "Politics or no politics, the Russians are totally antagonistic to England" were well remembered.

Besides, Victoria was not sure that the son of such an unfaithful family man and husband would prove any more worthy or devoted a husband, meaning Tsar's permanent relationship with Princess Catherine M. Dolgoruky. However, it was admitted that Sergei was a man of genuine culture, a gentleman in a European sense, being well read and passionately in love with music. Besides, deep in her heart Victoria had a strong suspicion that Ella was truly in love. In March 1884, Ella wrote to her grandmother: "I am so glad you will see Sergei when you come next month and *hope* he will make a favourable impression on you, all who know him like him and say he has such a true and noble character..."[5] She was happy when her engagement with Sergei was announced. "Dearest Ella looked so happy with Sergei, may she be so!," Victoria wrote to their grandmother on January 7th, 1884.[6] In giving her heart once, Ella gave it forever, though Hymen somehow misplaced the roses, and her future family life, as we shall see, did not justify her expectations.

To the outside world the bride and groom seemed a magnificent couple. But it would be hard to find two characters that contrasted so deeply. Ella's ravishing beauty, intelligence, delightful sense of humour, angelic patience and generous heart – all these gifts were hers. It was considered cruel and unjust that a woman of such virtues should have entrusted her future to *such* a person. Sergei was assumed to be the least popular of the grand dukes in Russia, irritating society and the Family by his obstinacy, ultraconservatism and anti-Semitism. Arrogant and disagreeable, he flaunted his many faults to the entire nation, providing the enemies of the regime with a rich source of material for calumnies and libels. Sergei's cousin, Alexander Mikhailovich* recalled in 1932/33: "Uncle Sergei played a fatal part in the downfall of the empire. Try as I might, I cannot find a single redeeming feature in his character."[7] The State Secretary A.A.Polovtsov called Sergei a "hypocritical saint" and thus described his behaviour at the sessions of the State Council: "...with a false look, with a strange grimace and sway of elbows drawn closely in towards his sides, he is concentrating on the idea of keeping an air of dignity, which is rather hindered by his failure in promotion, being just a colonel now, and not even a general-ADC."[8]

It seems that bad health had a dramatic effect on Sergei's character and formed his reputation as at best an eccentric. From early childhood the boy had to wear a corset, and suffered from the sneers and abuse of his elder brothers. Even in his manhood, he responded painfully when strangers noticed that particular garment. Felix Yusupov, who spent his childhood summer days close to Moscow, at the Arkhangelskoe estate, frequently encountered his august neighbours. He disliked Sergei because of his cold, arrogant manners, but got along very well with his wife Elizabeth. As a joke he liked to touch Sergei's corset stays, which could be seen through his white linen tunic, much to the Grand Duke's extreme irritation. During the years of their life in Petersburg, Ella realized the extent to which her husband was haunted and cornered by

* In the family and at court known as Sandro.

public opinion, and as a consequence, loved him more devotedly and passionately, as Russians say, "pitying" him (*zhaleia*).

...So the Department of Crown Lands and the Ministry of the Imperial Court began preparations for the wedding of this bachelor-member of the Imperial family. In December 1883, an order was issued "On the production of the holy icons for the blessing of His Imperial Highness on the occasion of His wedding".[9] Work proceeded at a high pace. On May 30, 1884, the Marshal of the Court received the following items for the approval: 1) the Image of Jesus (as on Veronica's Veil), an icon in a gold encasement, in a gold robe, with a halo made of precious stones (5,600 roubles), 2) the Image of Feodorovskaya Mother of God, with a halo of precious stones (4,399 roubles), and 3) a salt-cellar on a salver of gilded silver (1,000 roubles).

According to the order for "the manufacturing of precious items, fur, silver things, etc. on the occasion of the wedding of His Imperial Highness, and souvenirs for individuals",[10] in February 1884, "the diamond Order of St. Catherine, First Class, ‹12 at the price of 5 thousand roubles, a Robe made of Yakutia sables with a similar collar, all coated with velvet, and a boa and a muff all of sables, totalling 3,821 roubles" were made for the bride. A real wealth was submitted to Empress Marie Feodorovna for her approval. Those were necklaces, brooches, a fan of gold, china sets, porcelain and other necessary items, from hairpins and "shoes with a silk lining and trimming of swan down" to "silver ladies' travel kit with night-time accessories". However, the purchase of a private residence for Grand Duke Sergei was of the utmost importance.

The purchase of this palace in 1884, on the eve of wedding, was undoubtedly a stroke of good luck. The edifice, rebuilt by the illustrious architect Stakenschneider in 1846–48 after a fire, was located in the most desirable quarter of the capital: on the corner of the Nevsky Prospekt, that winter *rendezvous* of the fashionable world, and the Fontanka River, near the Anichkov bridge. This parcel of land had already been built upon during the reign of Peter I. The fine main house was steadily rising in price, and passed from one owner to the other. Finally in 1797, it was bought by Anna G. Belosselsky, the wife of Prince A. M. Belosselsky, an impeccable grandee, counsellor, senator, and the Russian Ambassador at the Dresden and Turin (Italy) courts. In the era of Emperor Paul, the prince was styled as Belosselsky-Belozersky, and his son Esper retained this title. In 1846, both mother and son passed away. The palazzo's next mistress became Esper's widow Elena (née Bibikov), who remarried to Prince V.V.Kotchoubey, an extremely cultured man and a passionate collector.

In a few short years, due to the magical skill of the architect Stakenschneider, who was an experienced revival stylist, the residence on the Nevsky Prospekt was drastically altered. It became the capital's first building decorated in the Neo-Baroque style. The facades were redesigned in the style of Rastrelli's Baroque revival of the mid-18th century. Its prototype, Count Stroganov's Palace, was situated on the same Nevsky Prospekt, on the intersection with the Moika River. The Belosselsky-Belozersky Palace ranked among the best and most beautiful of the capital's private homes, and the balls at the Kotchoubey's were the talk of all St. Petersburg. However, the colossal wealth soon melted away, and in 1881 the building was mortgaged, only to be repeatedly remortgaged in the following years. This made it possible for the Appanages Department to negotiate in favour of a sale to a royal person. The bargain went well. The palace was given a new name, the Sergievsky Palace, but the fast approaching, impending wedding only allowed enough time for the walls and furniture to be cosmetically freshened up.

In late May, 1884, Ella, accompanied by her father and younger sister Alix, set off to Russia to get acquainted with her future relatives. Their journey over most of Europe, with a stop in Berlin where the Hohenzollern hosts remained displeased with Elizabeth who had rejected two German suitors, finally brought them to the Russian border. The rest of the route to St. Petersburg was prepared and tended to in minute detail and at extraordinary expense, inconceivable by European standards, but habitual for the Romanovs. The railcars of the Imperial train, looking like an opulent palace on wheels, abounded in fresh fragrant white flowers, as Sergei knew that white was his bride's favourite colour. The train, decked out in the grand-ducal colours, ran at such a speed that the stations with their uniformed police and stationmasters standing at attention only flashed by. Their journey took them through Poland, and past Russian villages of log cabins and enclosures, all neatly aligned, past walled small towns with numerous onion-domed churches. At rare stops, civic administrations and the local notabilities bowed their respects, all in silk sashes and ribbons, awards and orders. The military in resplendent gold-embroidered full dress paid their respects, too; bands played; bearded prelates of venerable appearance, in velvet head-dresses, clad in shining vestments, blessed the travellers with gold crosses; the crowds of commoners cheered their delight and crossed themselves several times. Such a vociferous Russia stunned modest Ella and exceeded her every expectation. The arrival of the Princess of Hesse became a genuine sensation, when a few miles outside of St. Petersburg, at Peterhof, on the shore of the Gulf of Finland, the train came to a halt. Her fiancé Sergei, the Emperor and his family greeted the travellers at the station platform. The gilded magnificence of dozens of big and small residences, and the vast gardens with cascades and hundreds of fountains and marble statues far outstripped the grandeur of Windsor or Potsdam.

On June 2, 1884, the stately, regal entrance into St. Petersburg of Her Highness the Bride, arriving by a special train from Peterhof, took place. The royal party and numerous guests reached the railway station, where Princess Elizabeth followed Empress Marie into a gilt coach. Emblazoned with gold, the carriage of Catherine the Great, painted by the brush of François Boucher, drawn by eight grey horses, and led by gold-liveried postillions, proceeded from the Nikolaevsky railway station, and, after passing by Their Highnesses' private residence on the Nevsky Prospekt, pulled into the Palace Square. Everywhere crowds gave lusty cheers to Her Highness the Bride. The cavalcade drew up to the largest in Europe, magnificent Winter Palace, which counted over a thousand rooms and was inhabited by some two to three thousand people. On such a clear and superb festive day no one wanted to recall the appalling devastating fire, which had once gutted the Winter Palace; of the dynamite explosion staged by a terrorist in one of the dining rooms which spared Alexander II's life in 1880. Yet, a few months later, his mutilated body had been brought there after the next bomb explosion. All those gruesome events were forgotten as, to a salute by the Peter and Paul fortress guns, Princess Elizabeth stepped through His Majesty's entrance and was led up the marble Grand Staircase.

"Everybody fell in love with 'Aunt Ella' the very first moment she arrived in St. Petersburg from her native Hesse-Darmstadt. One evening in her company, and the memory of her eyes, her skin, her laughter, her genius for putting one at ease, threw us all into the depths of despair at the realisation of her approaching betrothal. I would have given ten years of my life to stop her from entering the church on the arm of haughty Sergei,"[11] wrote Sandro. But no miracle happened. The bride awaited her marriage ceremony joyfully, with a heart open to happiness, love, and fidelity to the grave. "I should be best man at the wedding of Uncle Gega,"* noted the future Nicholas II in his diary.[12]

The next day, the wedding took place, first in the Winter Palace's gold-flooded Grand Church, according to the Russian Orthodox rite, and followed by a solemn Te Deum. The high society at Church closely watched Ella's behaviour in anticipation of something odd to happen. Shortly before, in April, the regal bride of Grand Duke Constantine**, a German princess of Saxe-Altenburg, arrived St. Petersburg. To everyone's dismay, she refused to kiss the Orthodox cross after liturgy. "In contrast to Mavrikievna, the Bride [Ella] kissed not only the

* The family name of Sergei.
** Known as Grand Duchess Elizabeth Mavrikievna.

cross, but priest Yanishev's* hand. Her face is very appealing," admiral Ivan Shestakov recalled in his diary.[13] Then, at a ceremony in the white-blue stuccoed Alexander Hall of the palace, a prelate of St. Anna's church, pastor Freifeldt performed the Lutheran service for which he was presented with a wonderful ring. Ella was not required by law to convert to the Orthodox faith before marriage, which happened to many of her predecessors, as her fiancé was only the eighth in the line of succession to the throne. She was entirely at liberty to practise her own faith, and the patience and respect shown by Sergei to her allegiance forged their relationship. She voluntarily converted some time after, and this was to be an important factor for Alix, a Lutheran, to give her consent to marry the future Nicholas II.

Cheers, congratulations and souvenirs followed, and then a grand banquet was served in the largest Nicholas' Hall for persons of the first three ranks. In the gallery, an orchestra played, and the chorus of the Imperial opera sang under the baton of the conductor E. Napravnik. At nine in the evening, a ball began in the St. George's Hall, where the Emperor and the new-born H.I.H. Grand Duchess Elizabeth Feodorovna danced the first polonaise, and the Empress Marie Feodorovna with Sergei Alexandrovich followed next. The second round was performed by the newly-weds, as the leading pair, with the radiant Ella breathing happiness, her hand resting on the hand of her husband. All the singers and musicians were generously rewarded with gifts specially prepared beforehand.

The ball having finished there followed a ceremonial departure of Their Highnesses to their own residence where the guard of honour was installed. At 10:45 p.m. the young couple entered their home. On the landing of the gala staircase Sergei's brother, Vladimir and his wife (as their parents had died), in accordance with a Russian custom, welcomed them with an icon and bread-and-salt. In a drawing room near the concert hall, the couple received the Preobrazhensky regiment's guard

* The Emperor's private confessor.

officers with their souvenirs. At midnight, a family dinner was served for 36 guests. During the ceremonies, Ella had cheerfully borne the oppressive weight of her robe and jewelry. At last she could afford a short respite and thankfully retire, exhausted but delighted to be alone with her husband. The new grand duchess was exhilarated by the prospect of a private and intimate honeymoon. Its beginning is unresolved mystery. Days went on in a strange country of whose customs, religion and language she knew almost nothing. Soon the young people left for Iliinskoe estate near Moscow, allowing the overall refurbishment of the palace to begin in earnest.

On the way to Iliinskoe, the couple stayed over for a few days in Moscow, the ancient capital and spiritual heart of Russia. These days left a deep impression on the modest Hessian princess. The sight and sound of the bustling crowds was breathtaking. Everywhere over the roofs rose the golden and silver onion-shaped domes of the "forty times forty" churches. On Sunday, hundreds of church bells pealed out rich melodies. The beautifully furnished Nikolaevsky Palace in the citadel of Moscow, the Kremlin, where they were accommodated, the ancient architecture of the Tsar's frescoed chambers and temples, the solemn sanctity, and crowds of pilgrims enchanted Her Imperial Highness.

At Iliinskoe, whose park was the main charm of the estate, the couple lodged in a small two-story house, which had neither style nor pretensions. The estate, which Sergei had inherited from his mother, brought in nothing, and was in fact kept at a loss. He spent a great deal of money to maintain it. The annual whims of the owner were carried out without argument, however improbable they might be. For example, he once had rare prize cattle of a bright beige hue shipped in from Switzerland. On another occasion, he imported a rare Ardennes stud, becoming the only breeder of this pedigree in Russia. In Iliinskoe, something was always in the process of being built or reconstructed, including a new school, a greenhouse, an elaborate poultry house, and a cow shed.

The simple rural life on the couple's honeymoon, without stifling etiquette or official receptions, was quiet and relaxing. They rarely hosted picnics in the woods, but ventured into the fields alone to pick wild flowers, looked for mushrooms and berries, and rested by the riverside. Sergei helped his wife to study the Russian language, and she took classes diligently, each daily lesson lasting 90 minutes. Her tutor was Miss Catherine A. Schneider, who would eventually become tutor for the young Empress Alexandra, and, in 1917, she followed the Romanovs to Siberia. When dusk fell, Sergei read his newspapers. Ella leafed through English illustrated reviews or French fashion magazines. She cut out whatever pleased her or caught her attention and collected these pictures in albums for use in designing her own wardrobe. She also painted watercolour sketches. They usually retired early.

Here, in the tranquil atmosphere of Iliinskoe, Ella experienced a grave shock. Since their wedding enough time had passed, and her suspicions concerning her husband's physical interest in women became aroused. Would he ever sire her children? Would their marriage be just an empty formality? Did he find relations with her more a duty than a pleasure? What was wrong? Innocent and immature in her emotions, she probably had no idea of homosexuality, or that Sergei could have another kind of sexual desires. Without a devoted friend around, she was to cope alone with these horrific thoughts.

Too proud to complain of the worries and disappointments in her marital relations, Ella resolved to live an outwardly normal life and to keep up the facade of happiness. She had to fulfil the vows she made to love, respect and obey her husband. Although Sergei began to treat her as a child, she never challenged his will. Ella decided to love him for what he was, and, suspecting his torments of guilt, she now felt a strong protective streak of pity for one of nature's victims. As if trying to make up for the sorrows and wrongs he had inflicted, Sergei abandoned his cold arrogance and, in private, became more considerate and affectionate towards his wife.

Still, there was always duty before pleasure, as the Hessian princesses had been instructed since childhood. It seemed as if Ella plunged back into the habits of the life she had in Darmstadt, which included visiting poor families, bringing them food and provisions, and caring for the sick and unfortunate. The poverty of the Russian peasants and their shabby wooden huts, even on a grand-ducal estate, appalled the young mistress. She could not imagine that such poverty could exist in the world. The familiar German burghers and peasants, despite being ruined by continual wars, in her view, were so much advanced! Her husband quietly commented that all poverty was because of the drunkenness of the *muzhiks*. But he did not refuse to pay for many improvements. On Ella's request a trained midwife was installed in the village, and a hospital was built, as well as a school for boys. To the great excitement of the villagers, a few holidays and a fair were held. Ella liked the very tuneful but rather melancholy Russian folk songs, though to her surprise, the Russian folk dances were colourful, cheerful and even violent.

At the local village church, as well as in the ancient monasteries, the heart of Russian Orthodoxy, Elizabeth saw humble peasants praying with fervor, but found the reverence shown to the icons difficult to reconcile with her Lutheran faith. Where Sergei knelt and kissed them she made a very low curtsey, the custom to kiss the cross and the priest's hand was strange, but she did it as a mark of politeness. Her religion happened to be another unwelcome surprise making her behave and seem so different.

They would have preferred to continue this quiet life forever, but autumn was approaching. Sergei's leave was over, and he had to return to the Preobrazhensky regiment for the season of military drill and reviews.

On returning to St. Petersburg, Ella faced an entirely busy life: she had to do the honours as mistress of the residence of great magnificence. In their absence, capital alterations had been carried out, and a new church installed. On October 20, the church was consecrated, and Divine Liturgy was held within.

The choir of the Life-Guards Preobrazhensky regiment sang, and the liturgy was also attended by grand dukes Alexei, Paul, Constantine with his wife, and Pobedonostsev. October 20th was also Elizabeth's birthday and so Emperor Alexander III and his spouse arrived, had lunch, and then explored the palace, which had been transformed into a breathtaking sight.

The grand staircase, numerous drawing rooms and halls were decorated in the Baroque or Rococo styles. His Highness's private rooms were housed on the ground floor. To the right of the lobby, were located a reception and study, a bedroom and a dining room. These were Sergei's favourite rooms, as he greatly appreciated their decor.

In a small mosaic-lined dining room, the walls and ceiling were faced with light coloured nutwood, with the panels inlaid in precious wood. Two paintings on fruit and vegetable motifs added to the colour scheme. The upper part of the fireplace had a shell-shaped niche to keep an ivory Crucifix. Porcelain and antique ceramics highlighted this cosy dining room where Sergei played host to his closest friends alone.

The adjoining reception and study had an alcove for a sofa, which featured the wooden ceiling painted in oil in the Byzantine style. The alcove arch was coated in dark oakwood and had a carved double monogram under a crown at its apex. The monogram S & E was also featured over the fireplace. The study served for receptions of scientists and members of charitable societies. The Grand Duke was an honourable Trustee of the Imperial Lyceum, a patron of the archaeological institutions in St. Petersburg and Constantinople, Chairman of the Palestine Society, which assisted to restore Christian antique ruins and gave aid to Russian pilgrims who visited the Holy Land. At that time, in Palestine there appeared many Russian schools, hospitals, houses for the homeless, pilgrims and orphans. Russian Orthodox pilgrims could reach Jerusalem by using special benefits such as low price tickets, partly paid by the Society. The whole journeys, from St. Petersburg via Odessa and then by water to Palestine, would cost a quarter of an annual wage of a common worker, bed and meals being included. Before 1917, Jerusalem, Nazareth and Bethlehem had been visited by dozens of thousands of Russian peasants and craftsmen, let alone many wealthy pilgrims. Today, we can see in Israel many icons and all kinds of the church utensils, which had been presented by the Russian travellers of the past.

The metal guilded staircase balustrade, as ever when designed by Stakenschneider, is elegance itself, and features a monogram picked out in gold, leading to the first floor. This floor accommodated a number of gala drawing and dining rooms, as well as the private rooms of Her Highness. Among a few reception rooms, we should mention a concert hall in the late Rococo style, decorated with arches, pylons, caryatids and mirrors, which was often used as a ballroom. Always dressed with impeccable taste, dancing until dawn without a hint of weariness, Ella ranked amongst the *belle a ball* of St. Petersburg. Here she loved to dance with smart aides-de-camp of her husband, and Sergei helped to fill in her dance-card. He noticed that his favourite brother Paul, Ella's frequent dance partner, became too keen on Ella, and once asked her to be "less friendly". Even after having become a married man and a father, Paul never recovered from his platonic love for this *belle soeur* – which had already been noticed in Darmstadt – and his affection embarrassed and caused suffering for his young wife, Princess Alexandra of Greece.

The foyer was divided into three sectors by imposing figures depicting Atlas, and was well lit by five French windows. Its smooth plain walls made it ideal for use as a gallery. Sergei preferred the Italian masters, and bought a few small pictures for the Hermitage museum. He was as well as keenly selecting works by the Russian portrait artists of the 18th century for his private collection.

In the next library, a wooden gallery was built with balconies along the walls, and two ladders. Large two-headed eagles under a crown topped copper chandeliers, shaped as a massive church *panikadilo* for twenty candles. The library displayed marble busts of members of the Imperial family. His Highness was reputed to be an extremely well-read man, who kept a close eye on the latest historical literature and antique catalogues, always taking notes as to what he should obtain for his own library. Sergei managed to collect many letters written by Empress Elizabeth Alexeyevna, the consort of Alexander I. He intended to write a book about her.

The private apartment of the Grand Duchess was quiet and cosy, ornate in its Rococo splendour. Here Ella drew watercolour designs for her new dresses, and made preparations for approaching balls. It was her husband's wish that each new outfit should be matched with a special jewellery set, a field in which he was an accomplished connoisseur. After their engagement, he had literally showered exquisite gems on Ella, dressing her in a wealth of brooches, diadems, and necklaces, to the extent that she could hardly stand under their weight.

Her reception room, which doubled as a study, was upholstered in floral-patterned silks, with painted panels by the French artists of the 18th century, guilt trellis over the door lintels in the Rococo style, and a magnificent marble fireplace in high relief. Here Elizabeth used to write letters to Darmstadt, to sister Alix. The dormant artist in her, her sense of humour and refined taste are manifested in the design of these envelopes. Surprisingly this evidence of the touching tenderness and devotion between the two sisters has survived to the present time (letters in such envelopes are owned by remote descendants of the Romanovs in the USA). Each envelope is decorated with an original drawing: a floral motif, an amusing animal or a bird, comic episodes of the commoners' daily life. Evidently these drawings reminded Ella of German burghers, and they might be a hint of nostalgia, as if Elizabeth was pining for her native land. Russian characters and motifs had not captured her imagination.

She developed into a brilliant hostess, as Ella possessed a gift for creating an atmosphere of intimacy and gaiety under her roof, which attracted many friends and relatives to the Sergievsky Palace. The hostess always remained beautiful, delightful

Grand Duchess Elizabeth (Ella)

Queen Victoria
and her granddaughters
1879

Princess
Alice of Great Britain,
Ella's mother

Grand Duchess
Elizabeth, engraved
by Schübler after
a photograph
by Levitsky,
c.1890

Princesses
Irene and Ella of Hesse
and Victoria Melita
of Coburg (seated),
Alix and Victoria of Hesse
(standing) with their
husbands: Sergei, Nicky
and Ernst, c. 1895

Arrival of Princess Elizabeth of Hesse in St. Petersburg
Drawing by Brozh. 1884

Sergievsky
Palace (once
Belosselsky-
Belozersky
Palace),
at 41 Nevsky
Prospekt

Grand
Staircase,
a wrought-iron
balustrade
with Sergei's
monogram

Grand Duke Sergei Alexandrovich,
Governor-General of Moscow, 1901

Grand Duchess Elizabeth
wearing a court dress

Ella's green drawing-room

Rococo decorative details in Ella's
reception room, which doubled
as a study

A fireplace in Ella's reception room

Envelopes with Ella's drawings
mailed to Darmstadt for Alix. Private
collection, USA (first publication)

Theatrical perfomance at the Sergievsky Palace. 1888
Seated in the middle — Nicky, the Heir to the throne,
standing 3rd row, from left to right, 4th — Grand Duke Paul,
5th — Grand Duke Sergei. Ella in the centre

Theatre & Music Museum, St. Petersburg

Ella as Tatiana
Larina. 1890
Theatre & Music
Museum,
St. Petersburg

Scene
in the garden from
Eugene Onegin. 1890
Theatre & Music
Museum,
St. Petersburg

Grand Duchess Elizabeth as Mother Superior
of the Martha & Maria Community of Mercy
in Moscow

and charming, full of tact and grace, and, as always, kind to anyone, her kindness being not an artificial courtesy, but a genuine indulgent feeling. Prince Christopher of Greece recalled that at State balls she outshone every other woman in the splendour of her gown and jewels. When the ball was at her own house she had a habit of disappearing at midnight to change into a new dress and another set of jewels, then she would return to the ballroom more resplendent than before. She detested politics, political intrigues and discussions. Friends appreciated her inventiveness. In the midst of winter she used to initiate skating sessions on the garden lakes, sliding down an ice hill, and riding a *troika* in a sledge at a high speed through the snowed up alleys of Yelagin Island. "Was skating with Xenia and Aunt Ella. We had a good time romping and running about madly. Put on skates and played ball", was an entry in Nicky's diary.

In the middle of January, the traditional social *season* began, and it would end after Butter Week, when Lent followed in spring. At the Sergievsky Palace, balls were given throughout winter. "At 9 $1/2$, I go to the ball at Grand Duke Sergei's... The ball is rather colourful, with many people," Polovtsov wrote in his diary.[14] However, the Petersburg *beau monde* noted that it was not easy for these new hosts, in the same gala halls, to eclipse the glory and outshine the balls which had earlier been hosted there by Princess Elena P. Kotchoubey.*

Theatricals, tableaux, charades and costume balls in the Sergievsky Palace were also a great success. A unique photograph from 1888, featuring 23 individuals, has survived to the present day. It shows a costume ball or an amateur performance, very much in the fashion of many of the aristocratic salons of that era.

In general, the first matrimonial years were filled with theatre visits, amateur acting, the learning of roles and plays,

* She died at her new mansion in the Millioniers' Row in 1888. Until 1884 she still arranged balls in the palace on the Nevsky Prospekt which belonged to her son Constantine.

which required much care and enthusiasm. In the winter season of 1889/90, the finest performances were acknowledged to be *Boris Godunov* at the A.D.Sheremetev's, *The Tsar Feodor Ioannovich* by Alexei Tolstoy at Prince S.M.Volkonsky's and *Tsar Boris* by Alexei Tolstoy at the Hermitage Theatre. Staging it needed almost one hundred rehearsals. Costumes were mostly sewn at home, often by the aristocratic wives themselves. Performances were real fun, inspiring many amusing episodes and anecdotes. The "actors" spoke all too elaborately, they could not pronounce the consonant R properly (for example, Prince D. Gagarin would use 'G' instead of 'R'), and many joked that Tolstoy's tragedies seemed to have been written for russified Frenchmen, or for Russian Parisians.

Emperor Alexander III often attended the rehearsals of *Tsar Boris*, and gave advice and instructions, even, on occasion, performing himself. The spectators' curiosity was enhanced by the participation of a few august persons. Players included: Grand Duke Sergei as Tsarevich Feodor, Prince Peter of Oldenburg as a *stolnik* (a small role), Grand Duke Paul as Duke Christian of Denmark. The stage set amazed with its magnificence. The audience's gaze was caught by the Tsar's *ryndas* (bodyguards), wearing snow white tunic-caftans with gilded axes. The stage displayed some astonishing items, which had been taken from the Hermitage collection with His Majesty's permission. For example, they used a genuine saddle studded with turquoise and precious stones, which had been a gift to Tsar Boris from a Turkish ambassador. "A performance brilliant for the eye, as there were more diamonds than talents on the stage," commented the then Director of the Imperial theatres, Prince Sergei M. Volkonsky.[15] Many funny incidents and jokes occurred.

Once at a rehearsal, Count Neuhardt (then an officer of the Preobrazhensky regiment, and subsequently Governor of Odessa) when reporting the arrival of the foreign ambassadors, instead of "Miranda, Pope's nuntsii [nuncios]", announced: "Miranda, nuntsii Popsky." The following rehearsal he proclaimed the arrival of "nuntsii paptsii", before making matters even worse, to the delighted mirth of the audience. "Grand Duke Sergei alone, being responsible for that performance, frowned and asked Neuhardt to be more attentive next time." Alas! Too late! The performer could not muster his action, and whenever he approached that terrible phrase he would become confused and blurt out something improper. By dress rehearsals he was straying ever further from his mark: when reporting the arrival of the Swedish ambassador Erik Hendrikson he exclaimed: "The Ambassador from Sveya, Erik Nordenstrem," inadvertently giving the name of the most fashionable military tailor in St. Petersburg. Tsar Boris's courtiers creased up with laughter. The Tsar, in his *barma* and the cap of Monomakh, tried to hide his reddening face in a large red handkerchief. Only Tsarevich Feodor – Grand Duke Sergei – standing next to his father (who was roaring with laughter), remained gloomy and did not share the general intoxication of fun.[16]

In the palace, Ella and Sergei plunged into making the costumes. It is known, for example, that each costume for the numerous retinue of Christian, the Danish Duke, entailed expenses of 700 roubles (probably, more than $700 a piece). What was the cost of the costume for Tsarevich Feodor? Never mind the cost or the accounting! The essential point was to authentically reproduce the historical images. For this purpose the wives of the actors, the grand duchesses, borrowed ancient books with colour drawings from the library of the Academy of Arts.

Surprisingly Ella mastered the Russian language in two years to be often complimented on her proficiency. She spoke Russian both to her servants and Sergei (much unlike other German grand duchesses by marriage, or her sister Alexandra, who spoke only English to Nicholas II and her children, nor did her household hear any Russian from her). Admiral Shestakov noted in his diary on January 24, 1887, upon the end of his visit to the Anichkov Palace: "At lunch, my seat was next to Evgenia Maximilianovna and Elizabeth Feodorovna, who spoke in Russian to me. Fair enough."[17]

Elizabeth was soon able to perform, and not just a minor, third-rate role, but the leading ones. When extracts from *Eugene Onegin* were staged at the theatre at Tsarskoe Selo in 1890, Ella played the part of Tatiana. Tsesarevich Nicholas did the title role, not only having a passion for the poet Pushkin, but also secretly being infatuated by Aunt Ella. The scene in a garden, with Ella-Tatiana sitting on a bench, in a simple morning habit, her eyes cast downwards, stricken with horror at an unexpected encounter with her hero, that neighbour and Petersburg dandy Onegin-Nicky, was particularly well played. For Ella, understanding the poem's character posed few difficulties, with their shared longing for love and thirst to break free from the captivity of loneliness. But what about Nicky, in love with the spellbinding Ella? How difficult it must have been to lecture her on the merits of caution, on the dangers of innocence, and on the perils of unhappy marriage! "The young Grand Duke [Nicholas] showed an ...evident preference for Aunt Elizabeth Feodorovna. In winter, they met as a close family to rehearse parts from *Eugene Onegin*, but in essence they saw it as an exam in the Russian language for the Grand Duchess."[18] For Lamsdorf, that word 'essence' hinted at blossoming affection of the Heir to the throne. Soon, at his parents' will, Nicky was sent on a long trip to circumnavigate the globe, and to be rescued from the charms of the ballerina Mathilde Kshessinskaya.

Contemporaries, however, had their own opinion about the complex attitudes within the Imperial family and their young Hessian relative. "In the Gatchina theatre, I notice that His Majesty is letting the Empress go ahead, and Marie Pavlovna right after her*, and he himself is approaching Elizabeth Feodorovna, as he treats this *belle soeur* with great sympathy," Lamsdorf entered in his diary.[19] However, the Tsar soon cut short this kind attention, on noticing his brother's jealousy.

* Grand Duchess Marie Pavlovna, Sr, née G.D. of Mecklenburg-Schwerin. She was styled "senior" in 1890, when daughter Marie was born into the family of Grand Duke Paul.

In 1889, Lamsdorf wrote again: "Modesty and charm are as inherent in Grand Duchess Elizabeth, as they are lacking in her husband. Elizabeth was in no way created for the thoughtless genre of the reigning Empress, or Marie Pavlovna, etc. I think that the Grand Duchess must sometimes strongly sense the intellectual, moral and physical misery of her husband."[20]

Lamsdorf's comment is noteworthy. "A thoughtless genre" is an exquisite and somewhat mild definition of the high society's life style of the 1880s–1890s. Courtiers gossiped: "almost as in the times of Catherine the Great," pointing out loose morals, disloyalty, adultery, extreme debauchery, illegitimate children and piquant stories. Careers were made in alcoves. The moral barometer dropped, and such eternal virtues as love, fidelity, dignity, responsibility and mere decency were devalued. Most important royal relatives were in the lead of this entirely idle and dissolute life of the elite. Shortly before her death in 1960, Grand Duchess Olga of Russia had scornfully noted the fall of the dynasty's prestige: "No doubt that the last generation promoted the wreck of the empire. All those crucial years the Romanovs were not worth their rank or family traditions. Too many of us, Romanovs, had plunged in egoism where little mattered, except for infinite satisfaction of personal desires and ambitions. Nothing testifies to it better than the frightening marital disorder, which the last generation of my family took part in. Those incessant marriage scandals could not but have shocked Russia… But who of them cared of the impression which they made? Nobody did."

In St. Petersburg, the atmosphere of recklessness, restlessness, and obsession with sex appeared inimical to Elizabeth's upbringing. The young lady plunged into an entirely different world, which somehow shocked her. Ella was brought up in a sheltered puritan fashion *a la* Grandmother Queen Victoria, who was justly considered to have had one great love for her husband. Similarly Ella's mother Alice had a faultless matrimonial reputation and remained a guiding spirit, as did the late Empress Marie. Too inexperienced in daily trivial affairs, naive and ardent, longing to serve her new homeland and people, Ella was disgusted by the triviality of the shameful loud scandals.

The episodes from the lives of the Grand Dukes Constantine and Nicholas, Sr, who both developed permanent relationships with ballerinas and had illegitimate children, were common knowledge. The capital's gossips lovingly recounted Grand Duchess Vladimir and Zina Beauharnais to come to a ballet "in orange dresses as if both were courtesans". They twaddled about certain orgies which Grand Duchess Vladimir ("a very dissolute German")[21] afforded, as well as Countess Beauharnais, and a few others, when gathering in the palace of Grand Duke Alexei on the Moika River, at the Khitrovos', and so on. For weeks, busybodies amused themselves at a scandal at Cubat, a fashionable restaurant. During a supper with intimate friends in their *cabinet particulier* Marie Pavlovna insisted that a party in the adjoining cabinet would join theirs. The famous French actor Lucien Guitry was entertaining a group of male and female Bohemians there. Notwithstanding Guitry's protests, fearing all too accurately that their standards of behaviour would not fit the imperial status, they proceeded to supper together. Vladimir, who had drunk too much wine, seized Mlle Angele, Guitry's lover, and kissed her, which so enraged Guitry that he in turn put his arm about the Grand Duchess, and, it is said, even kissed her. Vladimir grabbed the actor about the throat, and soon close fighting began. The total disturbance was quelled by the timely arrival of the prefect of St. Petersburg. The next day the incident was reported to Alexander III, whose fury was beyond description. He issued peremptory orders that Guitry be sent out of Russia by the next train, and that Vladimir and Marie were to follow as quickly as possible.

At court, they talked about the scandalous *menage royal à trois*, and how, at the railway station, "Alexei Alexandrovich took an open carriage with Countess Beauharnais and was riding through the streets as if a married couple".[22] Another Ella's relative, Olga Feodorovna (Grand Duchess Michael), was not regarded as the most loyal of wives,[23] but being peevish and a gossip-monger. Olga admitted: "Many times I vowed not to speak badly about people, but could not constrain myself for more than three days." Grand Duke Nicholas, Jr. (Nikolasha), requested the Emperor's permission to marry a commoner, but was refused. However, he openly lived with his mistress and even received the subordinates in her house on the Vasilievsky Island. Grand Duke Michael Mikhailovich (Mish-Mish), obsessed with a desire to marry, tried more than once to marry morganatically. Ultimately, Emperor Alexander III had to make it a law that a grand duke that dared to marry morganatically was liable to be deprived of his grand-ducal rights and privileges.

The Court flirted recklessly, with scandal and danger, approaching that "plain insanity" that became characteristic of the first decade of the 20th century. In the opinion of the Russian aristocracy, the dynasty had long ago lost its halo of elegance and magnificence. Gone were the times when, in the reign of Nicholas I, there were only five grand dukes virtually regarded as demigods. In the late 1890s, in St. Petersburg, stuffed full with cringing state officials and military men, only two or three Imperial salons loudly trumpeted their pursuit of spiritual goals. In the lead were the hosts of the Marble Palace, Constantine (KR) and his wife Elizabeth Mavrikievna, and Helene and George of Mecklenburg-Strelitz. Alexander III's efforts to cement that frenzied society brought little fruit. The State Secretary and talented gossip A.A.Polovtsov wrote in 1889: "At a fish exhibition, half-naked peasant women were salting fish. Upon looking at them, the Emperor told Marie Pavlovna, that as costume balls were her well-known preference, therefore, she should use such a model for her next ball costume. In all, the attitudes between these two persons aggravate daily."[24]

Ella joined the world of the Russian aristocracy just on the verge of its collapse, when the symptoms were not yet obvious. The upper classes went on squandering money and dancing on the edge of the abyss, whilst the empire started falling apart, and the demise of that beautiful world was not far away. With Ella's acute sensitivity and strong spiritual goals she was too often never more alone than in the whirl of social life. "My strange, sad aunt," Marie Pavlovna, Jr., would eventually write.

Let us note a significant difference in the temperaments of the two Hessian sisters, Ella and Alix. It is customary to believe that Alix, after she became Russian Empress Alexandra, was still shy and timid, and only seemed cold and unsociable at court. However, the imperious and uncompromising Alix began her life in Russia with a hidden conflict with her mother-in-law, Empress Marie. In the Crimea, at the Livadia Palace, in the autumn of 1894, a few days before Alexander III died, she insisted that doctors and government officials should first report to her future husband Nicky about his father's illness. They were not supposed to hurry straight from the Emperor's bedroom to Empress Marie to deliver their reports. "Be firm and make the doctors come to you every day and tell you how they find him, so that you will always be the first to know. Don't let others* be put first and you let out. Show your own mind and do not let others forget who you are," she wrote in Nicky's diary.[25] A new attack soon followed on the Dowager, still exerting the full weight of her authority. According to the strict Court protocol and Russian tradition, a dowager took precedence over a reigning empress. At public functions Empress Marie, but not Alexandra, always walked first, on the Tsar's arm at the Winter Palace receptions. Alexandra followed in the second pair, on the arm of a senior grand duke, instead of on the arm of her husband, which caused much indignation, but the tradition was kept. Ella succeeded in avoiding any intrigues or conflicts, thus making for a stark contrast with her sister.

In the years of melancholy and loneliness, when the listless court life seemed a burden, she began searching in religion and charity for her rescue and consolation. Elizabeth raised considerable funds and spent much money on orphanages, old people's homes, on illegitimate children, donating towards the needs of senior citizens, invalids and the handicapped, on work-houses, and on a sobriety society. In 1888, she received

---

* "Others" implied Empress Marie Feodorovna.

the position of Guardian of the First School at the Imperial Female Patriotic Society, located on the Vasilievsky Island, where they established an initial class for training nurses, teachers and accountants.

The year 1888 became crucial, as nothing could conceal the lack of purpose in Ella's life. The glamour of the court life lost its novelty, her melancholy only increased in the whirl of entertainment. She was beginning to despair of ever bearing a child. A settled distant affection replaced her initial adoration of Sergei; the hopes of softening her husband's character had almost disappeared. Placid married life made her turn more often to religion as a guide and a consolation. It was a voyage to Jerusalem that enhanced her world of Christianity and filled her with new hopes.

In the autumn of 1888, the construction of a large Ortho-dox church of St. Mary Magdalene in Jerusalem, dedicated to the late Empress Marie Alexandrovna, was finished. Emperor Alexander III appointed his brother Sergei to represent him at the consecration. Elizabeth joined her husband. Together with Grand Duke Paul, the three of them journeyed to Kiev, where she admired the solemn majesty of worship in the ancient St. Sophia's and in the Monastery of the Caves. She watched the congregation, standing throughout the service for hours, the beholders crossing themselves with fervour, praying and singing in exultation. In compassion, she listened to the polyphonous chants of unaccompanied choirs that expressed intense religious feelings. Appeals for mercy, a plea of repent-ance, voicing fear, despair, happiness and bliss indelibly im-printed in her mind and soul.

The holy places in Palestine, the sites of the miracles and the very consecration of the Church of St. Mary Magdalene, at the foot of the Mount of Olives made her ponder about the true value of Orthodoxy. There, in the Garden of Gethsemane, her heart ached at the thought of the agony of Christ's prayer and His arrest. There on the Mount of Olives she urged to be at one with the people around her, with her husband, to share his religion and pray beside him and all of them. She had a sensational feeling that Orthodoxy offered her a new approach to God and would gain an intimacy with Sergei. She allegedly said, "here I would love to rest." She also realized how much Sergei was anxious for her to convert. But nearly three years flew before it happened.

In 1891, Ella converted to the Orthodox faith, retaining the name Elizabeth by choosing another patroness, St. Elizabeth the Pious, mother of John the Baptist. For such an occasion, an order was issued beforehand (1891) for "the procurement of a small cross for the day of baptism".[26] Following conversion to the new Orthodox religion, with each year Ella became more devoutly attached to its forms and practices. Although himself pious and scrupulous in observance of all the rites of Orthodoxy, Sergei watched his wife's increasing absorption in things spiritual with anxiety, and ended by regarding it as immoderate.

The emptiness in Ella's life that charitable deeds and religion could not entirely fill made her yearn for a close relative by her side. Ella missed Alix, often dreaming about her sister's marriage and arrival in Russia. At first, Elizabeth meant one of the numerous young grand dukes for her sister, but then she noticed Nicky's growing affection towards Alix. Together with her husband she tried her best to overcome the hostility of the House of Hesse, and more importantly, the strong opposition of Queen Victoria. In1887, the Queen wrote to her eldest granddaughter Victoria, Princess of Battenberg: "...my heart and mind are bent on securing dear Alicky for either Eddy or George.* You must prevent *further* Russians or other people coming to snap her up."

The negative attitude of Queen Victoria to any Russian fiancé has an obvious explanation. She did not trust Russia, regarding her as an uncivilized country, subject to anarchy and terrorism, as a place dangerous to the health of her granddaughters because of the terrible climate. "The state of Russia is *so bad*, so rotten, that at any moment something dreadful

* Eddy, Prince Albert Victor of Clarence. Georgie, the future king George V of Great Britain, in those years the Prince of York.

might happen and though it may not signify for Ella, the wife of the Heir to the Throne is in a most difficult and precarious position." The Queen emphasised that Russia was not liked in Germany, that the perspective marriage would produce a great division between all the families. In 1890, she wrote to Victoria of Battenberg: "...take care and *tell* Ella that no marriage for *Alicky in Russia* would be *allowed*, then there will be *an end of it.*" After Alix had visited Russia, Victoria informed her brother Bertie* that there would be no further marriages in Russia. On learning that, Bertie replied that Ella would move Heaven and Earth to get Alix to marry a grand duke. The Queen despaired, believing that Ella and Sergei were working behind the backs of Anglo-Hessian relatives, and encouraging Nicky's hopes. Besides, she knew the objections of Nicholas' parents who refused to allow such a union: the Emperor did not want further Russo-German family ties. Alexander III and Marie Feodorovna wished a daughter-in-law from a much grander, more impressive dynasty. They tried to arrange for a match with Princess Helene, the daughter of the pretender to the French throne, Louis, Comte de Paris. Then they sent matchmakers to Princess Margeret of Prussia, all in vain.

Ella tried to win her brother Ernie, who became Grand Duke of Hesse after his father's death, to her side. She convinced him of the incomparable virtues of Nicky, adored by all, how lovesick and lost the young man remained, having nobody in his family, except her and Sergei, to give him courage and hope. However, the first obstacle – Alix's change of religion, or religious pressures – had fallen in the wake of Ella's religious conversion. No doubt, Elizabeth repeatedly argued with her sister about the advantages of her new faith. In April, 1894, in Coburg, the wedding of Ernest Ludwig and Victoria Melita**,

* King Edward VII (1841–1910), during the reign of Victoria, the Prince of Wales.

** Victoria Melita, Princess of Saxe-Coburg and Gotha, divorced Duke Ernst of Hesse and married her cousin Grand Duke Cyril Vladimirovich, for which he was forbidden to return to Russia.

the granddaughter of both Queen Victoria and Alexander II, took place, bringing together a large number of royal relatives from all over Europe. Ella convinced Alix, who had previously claimed that religion was not a pair of gloves to be changed at will, that the Lutheran and Orthodox faiths had much in common. The second obstacle also failed to stand the test of time: in the Crimea, the Tsar fell gravely ill, he had incurable nephritis. The issue of the imminent succession became overriding. Reluctantly the Emperor permitted his son to marry.

Ella was nine years older than Alix, and felt a parental love and responsibility for her younger sibling, who had been always accommodated at the Sergievsky Palace during her visits to St. Petersburg. Sergei, together with his brothers Vladimir and Paul, went to Darmstadt, in 1894, to fix the engagement of Alix of Hesse to the Heir of the Russian throne. It was in truth Sergei, who, since 1887, had skilfully conducted the lengthy diplomacy of the engagement, and thus had presented Nicholas II with his treasure, his faithful life companion, the Empress Alexandra Feodorovna. Besides, Uncle Gega was a commander of the First (Imperial) battalion of the Preobrazhensky Guards regiment, in which the Tsesarevich served for a few years. This way Ella and Sergei won the special trust of the new monarch Nicholas II, and in the first years of his reign Ella helped her sister with advice.

The Hessian and English relatives knew that the grand-ducal palace on the Nevsky Prospekt was not a happy abode. Rumour had it that the marriage was a sheer formality, and that grand duchess's lack of an heir was not accidental. Sergei was accused of perverted tastes and unmentionable misdeeds. It was even alleged that the Grand Duke offered Ella to choose a "husband" from their close friends. As early as December 1, 1884, Admiral Shestakov entered in his diary: "Had dinner at the newly-weds. Just now finished reading a disgusting libel that the wife allegedly wanted to divorce Sergei Alexandrovich. She seems modest and a bit silly, but least of all she is a shrew."[27]

It would be churlish to make too much of insinuations about Sergei's instincts. However, memoirists repeatedly mention the constant companions and drinking mates of the Grand Duke amongst the young officers of the Preobrazhensky regiment, who were especially tender in their relations with him. Here is the opinion of David Chavchavadze, the author of the *Grand Dukes*, and Sergei's grand nephew: "He was singled out from all the others (grand dukes) by the scandal-mongers of St. Petersburg society, and was reputed by some to enjoy unmentionable vices. Current writers have been equally unkind, saying that he raped his wife, and thereafter they had no married life, accounting for the lack of children; that he was homosexual; that he was a sadist, enjoying torturing prisoners; that he indulged in sexual activities with both young girls and boys, particularly Jewish ones. There is undoubtedly an element of truth to these stories, but there is also no doubt that much was exaggerated. His brother, Emperor Alexander III, was very much the strait-laced autocrat, and it is doubtful that he would have appointed Grand Duke Sergei Governor of Moscow; nor that Nicholas II would have allowed him to become guardian of the children of Grand Duke Paul had half of these stories had any foundation in truth."[28]

Maurice Paléologue remembered Ella, whom he met in Paris about 1891, as a "tall, slender woman, with light, deep and naive eyes, a tender mouth and soft features, with harmonious and pure outlines to her body, with spell-bounding rhythm of gait and movement. Her conversation suggested charming female wit, natural, serious and complete kindness. At that time she was surrounded by mystery. Some peculiarities of her matrimonial life yielded no explanations". Many noted her inclination for solitude, using Sergei's severe, even despotic character to account for. Since marriage, he had become less intelligible, more suspicious and frequently jealous. He did not allow his wife to stay with anybody alone, or go out by herself. He read her correspondence and checked the books she preferred. He prohibited her from reading *Anna Karenina* for fear that the novel might provoke dangerous ideas. "An extremely cold person," as General A.A.Mossolov, Head of the court chancellery, commented. In the opinion of General N.A.Yepanchin, Sergei was "obstinate, stupid, arrogant, hard, cold and extremely susceptible to take offence, although he had an extremely high opinion of himself".[29]

Sergei's patronizing manner of addressing Ella as "my child", his annoying habit to exaggerate his drawl was much loathed in high society. Sergei "treated her rather as if she were a child. I believe that she was hurt by his attitude and longed to be better understood, but it was as if she were being driven deeper and deeper within herself for refuge. She and my uncle seemed never very intimate. They met for the most part only at meals and by day avoided being alone together. They slept, however, up to the last year of their life together, in the same great bed".[30] The final mention can be attributed mostly to their life in later years, in Moscow and Iliinskoe, when their foster-child Marie became a witness to it.

The short period of life in St. Petersburg (in all, 7 years!) had allowed Ella to take the measure of her earthly afflictions. The listless high life remained alien to her. The beloved man, sent to her by God, a deeply religious man, suffered from his personal predilections, and remained aloof, as if a stranger. Ella was embarrassed by Sergei's drinking bouts in the company of the Preobrazhensky Guard officers, which frequently began at the steps of the Sergievsky Palace staircase.* "The generals visiting the messroom of the Preobrazhensky regiment listened with stupefaction to the chorus of officers singing a favourite

* On drinking habits in the Guards see Massie, p.23, and *Diaries of Nicholas II*. About heavy drinking and homosexuality amongst guard-officers see Ed. Radzinsky, *Gospodi... Spasi i usmiri Rossiu*, p.28: "elbow" drinking (putting a wine-glass on one's elbow and then draining it from this distance), "ladder" drinking (a wine-glass placed on each step of a staircase, each of which would be emptied in a slow ascent, with many collapsing in a drunken stupor before reaching the summit) or "pretend wolves" (jumping naked out into a fierce frost, drinking champagne from a bowl, and then howling like wolves). "This terrible entertainment was proposed by G. D. Sergei who was known for drunkenness".

gypsy romance of Grand Duke Sergei, with its refrain consisting of the words – 'and peace, and love, and bliss'. The august commander himself illustrated those not very soldier-like words by throwing his body back, a tortured rapture in his features."[31]

Unfortunately, the Grand Duke was a poor officer who remained "indifferent to the Rules, and did not know any regulations, could not give a proper 'march' command and commanded on the left or right foot, at random".[32] We doubt Elizabeth was indeed proud of Sergei's soldiering.

Ella believed that her husband should always remain her first consideration. He was her Cross and her Destiny, and, like her mother-in-law, the late Empress Marie, she uttered neither reproach, nor accusation. Too proud to complain, Ella lived with Sergei for almost 20 years. She carried her lonely grievances and suffering to the grave. Her life in St. Petersburg had confirmed Her Highness in the submission to God's commandments, endowing her with calmness and self-possession, fortifying her will, which would rescue her in time of need, after the murder of her husband by a terrorist.

In 1891, Grand Duchess Elizabeth followed her husband to Moscow, where the Emperor appointed him Governor-General, ignoring Sergei's incompetence in domestic management. This assignment was completely unexpected, as Sergei learned of it for the first time on February 14th, at a ball in the Anichkov Palace. On February 26th, the highest order was issued.[33] Durnovo, the Minister for Internal Affairs, "has received from the Tsar an order, which was motivated as follows: 'My brother Sergei does not want to go to Moscow before it has been cleared of the Jews'."[34]

In the ancient capital, Sergei settled in the Governor's mansion, on Tverskaya Street, inconsiderately forcing out his predecessor, the widely popular and ageing Prince Dolgoruky. The Muscovites could barely stand Sergei's arbitrariness, haughtiness, and his tactless manners. We can only guess at how much the sensitive, kind Ella suffered from the behaviour and reputation of her husband. The Grand Duke had entered a drastically different world: Moscow remained "the city of pure leisure and the greatest freedom... Here everybody lives for oneself, according to one's own convenience, here in Moscow all thoughts do not gravitate to a single centre – the court, as in St. Petersburg".[35]

For fourteen years Sergei tried to tame Moscow "with an iron hand". In his sincere hope of punishing careless, inefficient officials or fraudulent shopkeepers through strict police measures, he often went about disguised as a private person, inspecting the real conditions in shops and offices, trying to catch the guilty red-handed. It is not known what the common people thought about these good intentions, but the Muscovite nobles, merchants and new industrial tycoons could hardly bear His Highness's roughness, tactlessness and arrogance. Sergei did not consider it wrong to refuse the Marshal of Nobility, who arrived to invite him to attend an important noblemen session, the reason being that he was taking a bath. He prohibited any traffic in rush hours on busy streets, as his carriage had been once caught in a jam there. He once failed to receive two important visitors at Iliinskoe. They were first told that the Grand Duke had been fishing for two hours, then that he had had dinner, and only after all that, were they informed that His Highness had no time, and they had to return to Moscow, in so doing losing a day. Having invited merchants, in order to persuade them to raise money for the benefit of the hungry, Sergei came out to meet them with a single glove on his right hand, which he allowed them to shake. In the face of such explicit contempt, many benefactors preferred to keep their money for themselves.

The coronation ceremonies in May, 1896, were blighted by the catastrophe in the Khodynka meadow, on the outskirts of Moscow. When food and mementoes were distributed to a crowd of half a million, panic broke out and a stampede occurred which took more than two thousand lives. It was first and foremost Sergei who insisted, with other ministers and advisors, that the Khodynka tragedy should be ignored and that the fabulous ball at the French Ambassador Montebello's not be cancelled. At that ball the monarch looked weary and ill at ease, and "seemed not pale, but just green". Sergei and the Minister of the Imperial Court accused and blamed each other for the disaster. Count Constantine von Pahlen, who was entrusted with the investigation as the former Minister of Justice, was to report before the Imperial family. He pronounced a fearsome historical verdict: "similar disasters will occur as long as Your Imperial Majesty will entrust responsible posts to such irresponsible people, as Their Imperial Highnesses, the grand dukes." Then all three brothers – Vladimir, Alexei and Paul – leapt to Sergei's defence and presented their resignation applications in the event of Sergei's trial coming to court. The matter was resolved with the dismissal of Colonel Vlassovsky, the chief of the Moscow police, and with junior officials bearing the brunt of the blame.

Count S.Yu. Witte recalled: "…[Sergei] essentially a rather noble and honourable person, but… due to limited ability and governmental inexperience, and on the other hand, an obstinate and stiff character, he employed stiff reactionary police measures in Moscow which greatly enraged every group of society… Unfortunately, he surrounded himself with incapable individuals with strong police instincts… he was devoted to extremely reactionary convictions with a nuance of considerable hypocrisy… thus he lost his life."[36] His Highness Grand Duke Sergei "played a fatal role in the downfall of the Empire," his cousin Sandro would say in the 1930s.

Life in Moscow was far less stimulating than in St. Petersburg. The Moscow high society included a handful of sybarite noble families far less flamboyant. Rich industrialists and merchants prevailed among the civic dignitaries. Ella parted from many old friends, including the Imperial family, and never obtained even a handful of devoted new ones. Wearing official duties of the Moscow governor's wife, entertaining, and pointless polite conversations made her so fatigued that she suffered from attacks of migraine. Nervous strain had to be carefully concealed, and Elizabeth gave her everlasting beauty the attention it deserved. In her memoirs Marie Pavlovna wrote of how her foster mother gave a great deal of time and attention to her appearance, and which face lotions she made with her own recipes. She did not permit the summer sun to touch her skin. She made a veritable ceremony of dressing for dinner or going out for a ball, the ritual including a fragrant bath, the donning of the complicated apparel of the period, manicuring, etc. The maids, the Mistress of the Robes, were all assembled to take part in this act of sanctity, never daring to break it by a minute of inattention.

Elizabeth came to visit St. Petersburg less and less often. "On January 22, 1903, 'all' St. Petersburg danced in the Winter Palace," wrote Sandro. "I remember the date, as it was to be the last spectacular ball in the history of the empire. The chief honours of the night were disputed between Ella and Princess Zinaida Yusupova. My heart ached a bit at the sight of these two 'mad devotions' of my early youth."

After 1902, Sergei and Elizabeth were appointed guardians to Marie and Dimitry, the small children of Grand Duke Paul. The latter was banned from the life and military service in Russia, as he dared to morganatically marry a lady without the Emperor's permission. Sergei loved his foster children. Ella hardly noticed them, they were more an annoyance than orphans to be loved and cared for.

…The Russo-Japanese war in 1904–05 encouraged an unprecedented growth in public activity in the rear, in aiding the battered Russian army. It gave an outlet for Ella's energy, and she put to use the compassion and charity that her new faith demanded of her. At her own expense Elizabeth organized several hospitals in Moscow, sending nursing units and ambulance railway cars to the front in Manchuria, organizing committees for widows and war orphans, and establishing a huge workshop at the Kremlin Palace where both commoners and noble ladies prepared linen and bandages for the hospitals.

Many writers described the last years of Ella's life, and there is little need to repeat them in detail. The tragic and horrific death of Grand Duke Sergei, who was killed at 2:40 p.m. on February 4, 1905, on the Kremlin territory by a bomb explosion, stands out as a black mark in the last pages of her life. The fatal bomb was thrown by a terrorist, Ivan Kalyaev. That explosion was so deafening that the windowpanes were shattered in the surrounding buildings, and Sergei's body was literally blown to bloody smithereens.

Elizabeth ran to the murder scene, arriving a few short moments after the calamity, by dashing out of the Small Kremlin Palace without a coat, wearing nothing on her head. In her heart she sensed a tragedy, and she was running across the snow in her light shoes, stumbling, falling and sobbing in grief. The crowd did not want to let her through to the scene of the accident, where little had been left of Sergei's body – a fragment of torso, a leg, a torn off hand. The Grand Duchess vainly searched for her husband's head and his breast cross. She picked up pieces of his body and clothes, a few of which were found on the rooftops of the nearby buildings. The coffin was filled with these bloody, headless remains.

Stricken with grief, Elizabeth could hardly stand. Nevertheless, several times she demanded news of her husband's coachman who had received 79 wounds and lay in a hospital, fighting for his life, his body torn by the same bomb that had killed Sergei Alexandrovich. Toward 6 p.m. Ella went herself to visit the wounded man; and, in order not to dismay him with signs of open mourning, she kept the same light blue dress she had worn all afternoon to the hospital. When the coachman asked for news of Sergei's health she had the courage to reply with a smile that it was the Grand Duke himself who had sent her to visit him. The poor man died peacefully during the night.

Elizabeth demonstrated evidence of an almost incomprehensible heroism. Princess Zinaida Yusupova telegraphed to Petersburg that Ella "was bearing her terrible grief like a saint!" Always confined within herself, she became more so. Only her eyes, and sometimes the beaten look on her face, betrayed her suffering. The long years of almost complete passivity gave way to an unexpected explosion of energy. In 20 years of married life she had given no orders in the house, where her husband had ruled supreme. Now she herself took charge of all the grisly, painful details of the funeral. A memorial cross was erected with an inscription on the spot that marked the assassination. Designed by the artist Victor Vasnetsov, it read: "Forgive them, Lord, for they do not know what they do". It was these words that Ella would repeat on a July day, 1918, as she faced death at the hands of the Bolsheviks.

Sergei was buried at the Chudov monastery. Only two members of the Family attended the funeral: the rest were afraid of subsequent terrorist acts. Constantine (KR)* took the risk and arrived from St. Petersburg, and the exiled Paul was allowed to visit from abroad for a few days. Also at the funeral were the Grand Duchess Marie of Saxe-Coburg** with her daughter Princess Beatrice, and Ella's relatives, the Grand Duke of Hesse (Ernie) with his wife the Duchess Eleonora, Princess Victoria of Battenberg, and the kind and courageous Duke George of Mecklenburg-Strelitz. At Requiem, the coffin was strewn in wreaths and garlands, and the services were held from morning to night, without interruption. The public was allowed in to pay its respects, a hundred people being let in at a time. Her Highness ordered that the people were in no way constrained or interfered with, and they were given free access to the Kremlin.

"...Those weeks of sorrow brought us closer together and we had long intimate conversations," their step-daughter Marie recalled. "In one of these talks she confessed to me that she had suffered a great deal because of the affection which my uncle had shown us so completely...She acknowledged herself guilty of brusqueness and injustice, born of that jealousy; and set herself now to make amends, attaching herself particularly to my brother, who was my uncle's favourite."[37]

* "A longing to pay tribute to a cousin and personally express condolences to a widow," KR wrote in a diary. His brothers, who remained in St.Petersburg, regarded the matter differently. They said that KR "betrayed them, for his presence at the funeral highlighted their absence" (Passion, 218).

** Sister of G.D. Sergei, daughter of Alexander II.

Elizabeth went to visit Sergei's murderer, the 28-year-old Kalyaev, in prison, which caused horrendous dismay within the prison's administration: nothing of the kind had happened before. She insisted on being left alone with the murderer, and gave him an icon. On the eve of the visit she had a vision: on the night 5th of February, Sergei appeared and told her that he had forgiven the murderer and asked her not to condemn Kalyaev. Ella wanted to plead for a pardon from the Emperor, but Kalyaev wanted to die as a hero. To him, the idea of dying in assassination attempt or of being executed for his beliefs was a heroic martyrdom. He replied with a letter that was shocking in its disrespect. The letter was never shown to Ella. It was at this time that the Grand Duchess decided to leave her secular life. Released from the bondage of her marriage, she gave way to an intense urge to ease the sufferings of other people.

In 1909, Elizabeth ended her mourning and put on the attire of a nun, dismissed her court in the Kremlin, pensioned off her servants, and devoted herself to the service of God. Her property was distributed between the treasury, her heirs and charities. Her WILL[38], as being signed by the Emperor, countersigned and sealed in 1911, is a fascinating detailed document of 11 vast pages. Its part ONE had it: Elizabeth's personal belongings, pictures and china sets, which remained at the Nikolaevsky Palace in Moscow should be shared among her brother and two sisters living abroad, and to be duly inherited by their heirs. All wealth of the Sergievsky Palace, and Iliinskoe and Ussovo estates should be inherited by her nephew Grand Duke Dmitry. From September 1911, the Sergievsky Palace became property of Dmitry. She also assigned the sum of 275,000 roubles to her niece Marie Pavlovna for building the new palace in Stockholm. All jewels belonging to Empress Marie Alexandrovna, and inherited by Sergei, she had earlier returned as *fidéicommis* to Alexei and Paul Alexandrovichi. Her own money, bonds and proceeds from the real estate was bequeathed for charity and for the needs of the Community and its inhabitants.

She built the Community of Mercy of Martha & Mary (*'Obitel'*) for prayer, work and charity. By naming her new community after Martha and Mary, Elizabeth emphasised that she wished to combine in her labours the service of Martha who was 'careful and troubled about many things', and she received Christ into her house. Mary epitomised the sense of listening and contemplation, as 'she sat at Jesus' feet and heard his word'. Her daring innovation was to found a sisterhood of nuns dedicated to nursing and charity. Traditional Russian convents neither taught nor nursed. They led a strictly contemplative and severe life, and the nuns would leave their enclosure in very rare cases to beg for alms.

In 1910, the Moscow Metropolitan Vladimir consecrated her as Mother Superior of the Order that she created. She suggested the restoration of the ancient order of female diaconate, which had been quite widespread in Byzantium, but disappeared from church practice in a medieval world, when the inferiority of women had been increasingly taught by religious institutions. She did not dare to damage relations with the Holy Synod, the bulwark of conservatism. Yet, conflicts arouse. Then Nicholas II had to intervene and ask the Synod to leave his sister-in-law in peace. Elizabeth and 17 sisters were unofficially ordained to the diaconate in a special manner: the service of dedication did not take place during the Eucharistic liturgy, when men are normally ordained to the diaconate or priesthood, but in the evening, before the end of vespers.

With a last touch of worldliness, for she had been a woman of extreme elegance and great taste, she had the habit of her Order designed by Mikhail Nesterov. Muscovite artist Nesterov remained unique in depicting Russia in prayer in his paintings. He created a long pearl-grey robe of fine wool, a lawn wimple, which framed the face, and a white woollen veil that fell into long classical folds. Elizabeth and her sisters hardly ever wore black habits. For feast days they wore white, and on ordinary days light grey. Eventually Elizabeth faced death wearing that sisterhood habit.

The Mother Superior lived the Spartan life of a hermit. Her wooden bed had no mattress and her pillow was stuffed with hay; she slept for three hours at most, observed the fasts, and prayed in the chapel. Annually, the community received more than twelve thousand applications and requests, and sent off 300 dinners a day to homes for the poor and destitute. The finest doctors treated patients free of charge in their hospital and ambulance station, all the sisters had to take a basic medical course; there was a dental clinic and a pharmacy as well. Elizabeth took in more orphans from the filthiest areas, cared for the sick, and visited the poor. The Grand Duchess set up a women hostel, homes for cripples, expectant mothers and old people. She believed that such work might be a model to follow in other parts of Russia. Many a contemporary reiterated that there was holiness without a hint of hypocrisy about her, so much simplicity and sincerity.

On Sunday, after vespers, discussions on faith were organized in the Sisters' church to stimulate people to think about their faith, and not only to say their prayers. Bishops and other prelates arrived. In all, such a bold novelty was frowned upon or condemned as a Protestant deviation.

Seven hundred years later, the story of St. Elizabeth of Hungary, Ella's ancestress after whom she was named, repeated once again. She also married a foreigner and lived in a strange country, entered a holy order after his death, rid herself of the wealth and used it for the benefit of the poor and afflicted. Like her, Ella found her ideas sneered at court and by the society, and herself being highly venerated by people, finally to become a saint.

In August 1914, the war broke out. Russia, France and Britain fought against Germany and Austria, which became an immense personal drama for Elizabeth, who was German on her father's side, English on her mother's, and Russian by adoption. She organized field hospitals at her own expense, by using finance paid to her as a grand duchess from the Appanages Department. Like her mother Princess Alice, during the first weeks of the war she visited hospitals, comforted the wounded, collected medicines, gifts and warm clothes for Russian soldiers. But as she attended to the needs of German and Austrian PWs as well, gossip in Moscow made out that she was a spy for the enemy. Her relations with the court and the Tsar's family had become strained during these last years.

In the summer of 1915, hostility towards persons of German origin, caused by the defeats suffered by the Russians on the frontline, reached its peak, and in Moscow it brought dangerous unrest, and verged on rioting. *Pogroms* (looting) of all shops bearing foreign signs occurred in many areas. Then huge mobs began plundering Russian wine cellars, and worse, the private apartments of individuals who had lived in Moscow for generations, their arrival dating back further than living memory. They owned important businesses and had already forgotten their Germanic origins. This pillage was watched with complete indifference and inaction from the government and the police. "All the windows in the Nikolaevsky Palace had been smashed, because a drunken mob believed that Grand Duchess Elizabeth was hiding her German brother, Grand Duke Ernst of Hesse, there. He was rumoured to have secretly come to Russia to negotiate a separate peace settlement."[39]

"There was particular ill-feeling and rage against Ella," Natasha reported*, "because everyone knows how she cares about the German prisoners of war." Soon the German Ambassador to the Soviets, Count von Mirbach, suggested Elizabeth Feodorovna to depart for Germany. Cousin Kaiser Wilhelm had not forgotten his rejected love. Ella's answer was extremely brief: she would never, of her own free will, leave, neither her convent, nor Russia. Mobs occasionally appeared at the community walls, but shouts, threats and insults did not frighten her.

* Natalia Sergeievna (Natasha),Countess Brassova, née Sheremetievskaya, daughter of the Moscow lawyer, a morganatic wife of G.D. Michael Alexandrovich. Her first husband – Sergei Mamontov, a musician, pianist with the Bolshoi Theatre; her second marriage was to Vulfert, a cuirassiers-guard.

Marie Pavlovna, Jr., recalled in her *Memoirs*: "Towards the close of 1915, early in December, I visited my aunt Ella in Moscow... [she] had greatly changed during the last few years. In spite of the fact that she was living in a nunnery, she came now into contact with a greater number and variety of people. This had broadened her outlook, made her softer, more human."[40]

Elizabeth emerged from seclusion and arrived in St. Petersburg in April 1916. In Nicholas' II Diary, dated April 18: "...Ella arrived at breakfast and will stay for 1,5 days"; then, an entry of April 19 "Ella had breakfast", "Had dinner with Ella and Dimitry. At 9 $\frac{1}{2}$, she left for Moscow". These sparse notes conceal an infinite world of lost hope, alienation, and a split in the family.

In Tsarskoe Selo, Alexandra expected her elder sister's arrival with fear. She had a presentiment – the conversation would concern Rasputin. Just recently, the former governess of the grand duchesses at Tsarskoe, a lady-in-waiting named Sophia Ivanovna Tiutcheva, visited Ella in her convent. Tiutcheva stated that *starets* [Rasputin] would go into the nursery praying along with the Tsar's daughters Olga and Tatiana, sit there talking to them while they were getting ready for bed, and caressing them. The governess reported everything to the Empress, and in a few hours she was dismissed.

Elizabeth tried to make her sister aware of her blindness, pointed out that Rasputin was a fraud and a lecherous drunkard who rankled society, compromising the Imperial family and leading the dynasty towards ruin. At the first mention of Grigory's name, Alexandra became stiff and isolated, and asked her sister to have mercy for a "man of God". They parted as a ruler and a subordinate – dry, cold, officially. As Pierre Gilliard recollected: "A few hours later, the Grand Duchess left for Moscow in horror. The Empress, with her daughters, saw her off to the station. The sisters bid each other farewell; an unfailing boundless tenderness had remained between them, which had connected them from childhood, but they understood that something between them had been torn."

In December 1916, the Family members convinced Ella to once again try to talk to her sister, but the conversation immediately led to an impasse. Alexandra blank-pointedly refused to speak about Rasputin. "Remember the fate of Louis XVI and Marie Antoinette," was Ella's final attempt at persuasion. At these words Alexandra got up, picked up a telephone receiver, and ordered a car to take Ella to the station. "I probably shouldn't have come," Ella said sadly. "No," agreed Alexandra. It was their last meeting.

Felix Yusupov recalled Ella's last visit: "Later the Grand Duchess, who appeared very rarely at Tsarskoe Selo, made a last attempt to convince her sister. She promised to come and see us on leaving the Alexander Palace. We all waited eagerly for her arrival, anxious to hear the result of the interview. She entered the room trembling and in tears: 'She drove me away like a dog!', she cried. 'Poor Nicky, poor Russia!'."[41]

Anna Vyrubova, Alexandra's bosom friend, wrote that all secret correspondence on Rasputin's murder among the relatives was seized by the police and reported to the Empress, and the effect was devastating and stunning. "Without knowing the details of the murder, Ella has sent an enthusiastic and careless cable to Dimitry, which was brought to the Empress's attention (Ella was accused of conspiracy – Z.B.)… Some time later, the Grand Duchess sent her sister a few sacred icons from the shrine of Saratov. Without looking at the gift, the Empress ordered them sent back to the Martha and Mary Community."[42]

In June 1917, Maria Pavlovna went to Moscow where she stopped at Ella's nunnery. She left a memorable account of that visit. "I had not seen my aunt for several months. Nothing around her had changed, the atmosphere was still the same, but I was struck by her tired and ill appearance. She, who had always been on the go, now spent most of her time upon a wicker chaise-longue with a piece of embroidery or some knitting. We talked at length of present events and of the causes that had brought them about. One evening when I was telling her about the life of the captive Emperor and his family, I added that if she wished to send them a letter, I might find the means of having it delivered. Her eyes turned hard and cold, her lips tightened. She replied somehow sharply that she could not send a letter; she had nothing to say; she and her sister, the Empress, had long ago ceased to understand each other."[43] Maria and Ella never saw each other again.

In August 1917, under the headline "In the Romanov Family", the Crimean Bulletin published the following article: "The Grand Duchess Elizabeth Feodorovna, who lives at the Martha and Mary convent, has addressed the Commissioner of the Provisional Government in Moscow, N.M.Kishkin, for an explanation, as to whether it is necessary for her to make the new government a formal declaration of submission to the existing order. The appeal of Elizabeth Feodorovna was supported with an indication of the fact that she had recently torn off any relation with Court, mainly, on the grounds of disputes on the matter of Rasputin. N.M.Kishkin recommended the Grand Duchess to write directly to the Head of the new government, and thus to determine her attitude to the new political order. Elizabeth Feodorovna telegraphed G.E.Lvov, Minister-Chairman of the Cabinet of ministers, of her submission to the new government. She also asked for permission to continue charitable work in Moscow. Yet in the beginning of events, the new Moscow authorities decided that Elizabeth Feodorovna should settle in one of the Kremlin palaces. But she asked to remain in the Martha & Mary convent, in Small Ordynka Street, where she stays all time and never leaves it. Formally the Grand Duchess is not under arrest, but at the gates of Martha and Mary convent sentries have been installed for protection."

In spring, 1918, at Easter, events took a gloomy turn when the orphans were taken away to other orphanages, the sick were arrested by the VCHeKa, and in June, Mother Superior was escorted to the Urals. Ella quickly collected her simple possessions and immediately prepared for departure in the company of the two Sisters, Varvara Yakovleva and Yekaterina Yanysheva. She was told that the former Emperor Nicholas II, who had been deported to the Urals, wanted to see her. Felix Yusupov writes in his memoirs that Patriarch Tikhon tried, in vain, to trace Elizabeth and release her. At last, it became known that she was a captive in Alapaevsk in the Perm district, a hundred kilometres from Yekaterinburg. She was spared misfortune to see or to hear how on May 1, 1918, Lenin and Sverdlov, in person, had a loop thrown over a monument to her husband Sergei Alexandrovich and smashed it down to the ground, accompanied by the enthusiastic cheers of the crowd.

She was brought first to Perm, then further to the Urals, where she joined other captives: Grand Duke Sergei Mikhailovich, Princes Ioann, Igor and Constantine Constantinovichi and Prince Vladimir Paley*. The last rooftop over Elizabeth's long-suffering head happened to be a school in Alapaevsk. On July 18th, she was thrown down a deserted mine shaft together with five other Romanovs. The murderers subsequently reported that it was the old woman in monastic clothes that had stepped on to the mine's edge first. She crossed herself with a cross and repeated the words: "Lord forgive for they know not what they do". Covering her head with a coverlet, chanting her favourite Cherub's song, she disappeared into the depths of the shaft. The executioners threw grenades and dynamite down into the pit after them.

Following the White army of Admiral Kolchak entry into the town, an investigation was carried out, and inspectors extracted the bodies of those Romanovs that had been thrown down the shaft alive. Prince Ioann's body had a wound that had been dressed with a kerchief. It seemed that the Grand Duchess, with broken limbs and awful bruises to her head, had tried to give comfort to the young man suffering nearby. The relatives were later told that the bodies of Elizabeth and Vladimir Paley, who had died of hunger and thirst, were found lying next to each other.

All seven corpses were placed in the burial vault of the Holy Trinity Church in Alapaevsk, and thereafter transferred to Chita (Siberia) with the help of Father Seraphim. Finally the coffins reached the Russian Orthodox Mission in Peking. Father Sera-

* Son of Paul Alexandrovich, born out of wedlock, nephew of Elizabeth Feodorovna.

phim started from Alapaevsk in July 1919, and arrived Peking in April 1920. Later, in 1920, the Hessian relatives, Ella's elder sister Princess Victoria, the Marchioness of Milford Haven, had so arranged that the coffin with the remains of the fearless Elizabeth was transferred to Jerusalem, along with the remains of the devoted nun Varvara, who had died in the same mine.

Legend has it that four years after their marriage, when Elizabeth and Serge visited Jerusalem, on viewing a wonderful church she allegedly exclaimed: "Here I would like to lie." Many years after, right there, in the Orthodox convent, in St. Mary Magdalene church on the Mount of Olives, the Grand Duchess is resting in peace.

However, the Will & Testament[44] of Grand Duchess Elizabeth Feodorovna, testifying her sole wish, was authorised by the Emperor, and dated June 4th, 1911: "I request that I be buried in a crypt… of the Church of Our Lady's Shrine which I built on my own land property, in Bolshaya Ordynka Street, Moscow, at the Community of Mercy. A special place has already been arranged, and it is known to Father Mitrophani and Mother Superior." Elizabeth specified the features of entombment in great detail. Her Will ended with a request that wreathes should not be lain on the tomb, nor on the catafalque, nor on her grave. Instead, the money would be better used if offered for the Community's needs.

From 1946 to her death in 1970, there lived as Mother Superior of St. Mary Magdalene convent in Jerusalem another noted member of the Imperial family. The pious Sister Tamara had once been a beautiful Princess Tatiana Constantinovna, daughter of the celebrated poet KR. She had quite a tragic destiny. Her first husband, Prince Bagration-Mukhransky of Georgia, was killed in the WW I. Tatiana was left with two small children on her hands, and soon they were impoverished by the revolution. The family escaped from Russia in 1918 via Odessa, then Rumania, and finally Tatiana settled down in Switzerland. Her second married life was a failure: in 1921 she married a colonel Alexander Korochentsov who died in 1922.

In 1984, the Russian Orthodox Church Abroad had canonized Ella, before and apart from the other Romanov martyrs. In 1992, Elizabeth Feodorovna was canonized by the Orthodox Church of Russia. A statue of the Grand Duchess Elizabeth has recently been erected on the exterior of Westminster Abbey in London together with those of other 20th century martyrs. Another statue of her, sculptured by Klykov, has been shortly erected on the grounds of her *obitel'*, the Martha and Maria Convent in Moscow. At present, with the blessing of Alexii II, Russia's Patriarch, a special Canonization Committee has begun the work of drawing up a narrative of her life.

REFERENCES

1 A.M., p.160
2 Polovtsov, vol.2, p.160
3 Tolstaya, p.133
4 Lamsdorf, p.90
5 Almedingen, p.18
6 Almedingen, p.17
7 A.M., p.158
8 Polovtsov, vol.2, p.307
9 RGIA, *opis'* 431/1565, *delo* 149 (1884)
10 RGIA, *opis'* 432/1566, *delo* 149 (1884)
11 A.M., p.159
12 Passion, p.10 (28 May, 1884)
13 Shestakov, *fond* 26, *opis'* 1, No. 4
14 Polovtsov, vol.2, p.306
15 Volkonski, vol.1, p.44
16 Volkonski, vol.1, p.44, 45
17 Shestakov, *fond* 26, *opis'* 1, *delo* 7
18 Lamsdorf, p.304
19 Lamsdorf, p.20
20 ibid, p.207
21 Bogdanovich, p.81
22 Polovtsov, vol.2, p.192
23 Witte, vol.1, p.419
24 Polovtsov, vol.1, p.170
25 Massie, p.42
26 RGIA, *opis'* 501/2191, *delo* 44 with a note 'vybylo'
27 CG VMA, *fond* 26, *opis'* 1, *delo* 5
28 Chavchavadze, p.119
29 Yepanchin, p.211
30 M.P. Education, p.17
31 A.M., p.159
32 Yepanchin, p.219
33 Bokhanov, p.42–45
34 Polovtsov, vol.2, p.372
35 Tiutcheva, p.112
36 Witte, vol.2, p.320
37 M.P. Education, p.73
38 RGIA, *fond* 468, *opis'* 46, No. 136, 9 l.l.
39 Crowford, p.191
40 M.P. Education, p.443
41 Yusupov, p.168
42 Passion, p.513
43 ibid, p.577
44 RGIA, *fond* 468, *opis'* 46, ll. 7–9

The Crimean Captives

*…I am particularly choosy, particularly
mistrustful, in my attitude towards a Russian
in power. Not long ago a slave himself,
he quickly becomes the most unrestrained
of despots, as soon as he has the chance
to be the master of his nearest and dearest.*

Maxim GORKY, *1917*

In the early spring of 1917, the Romanovs found themselves
in the Crimea, for the first time out of season, and against their
will. After Nicholas II's abdication in Pskov, on the 2nd (15th) of
March, 1917, an event that was to have tragic and fateful
consequences both for his family and his relations, and for the
Russian people at large, the Romanovs became scattered.

The grand dukes Nikolaevichi arrived in the Crimea first,
in the middle of March 1917. They were Nicholas Nikolaevich,
Jr., with his wife, Anastasia Nikolaevna (Stana), and his
brother, Peter Nikolaevich, in the company of his wife Militza
and their children, Marina, Nadezhda and Roman. Stana's
grown-up children by her first marriage, Sergei and Yelena of
Leuchtenberg, came with. The retinue of the former Supreme
Commander included his adjutants, Princes Vladimir Golitsyn
and Nicholas Orlov, and Stana's secretary, Boldarev.

Nicholas Nikolaevich (Nikolasha) arrived straight from the
Headquarters (*Stavka*) at Mogilev, where he had come on the
10th of March on a train from the Caucasus. He did not know
that he had already been dismissed. Only on the following day
did he hear the disheartening news that, by a special decree,
the Provisional Government had cancelled his reappointment
as commander-in-chief, signed by the Emperor on the 2nd of
March, just prior to his abdication. The document appointed
General Alexeev to the post, and prohibited members of the
Romanov family from further service in the army or navy.

On the same day, the 11th of March, Nikolasha sent a telegram to Prince Georgi E.Lvov, the new Prime Minister, informing him of his resignation and the termination of his oath of allegiance to the Provisional Government. A second telegram was sent to Guchkov, the Minister of War, notifying him of his resignation, transferring his supreme command to General Alexeev, and requesting the right to wear his military uniform, as befitted a recipient of the St. George Order, First Class. Peter and his son, Roman Petrovich, a prince of Imperial blood, whose military career was unexpectedly cut short, quickly followed his example. He had served all of six months. The close relatives of Nikolasha that were escorting him, Prince Alexander of Oldenburg and Sergei Duke of Leuchtenberg also resigned. For two or three days they waited for an answer to Nikolasha's request to be allowed to retire to his Crimean estate, and to live there as a private individual.

A permission and order to move to the Crimea, with an escort of two members of the State Duma, finally arrived at Mogilev. Both of the governmental commissars, one a member of the Cadets party from Ufa, and the other – a liberal from a Moscow faction, travelled on the Grand Duke's train. The departure of the military leader, so recently idolized by the army, and his conversion to civilian life, was not officially marked with any pomp or ceremony. Several high-ranking military officials, and General Alexeev himself, came to bid him farewell in his carriage. The train pulled out. The sternly silent Nikolasha made the sign of a cross. Never before his future seemed so gloomy and overcast. In Kharkov Nikolasha and Peter were joined by their families who had journeyed from Kiev. From the Crimean railway station Nikolasha and Stana travelled on to their estate, Tchaer. The *Crimean Herald* noted:

> The former Supreme Commander Nicholas Nikolaevich Romanov arrived at Belbek Railway Station yesterday morning, from where he journeyed to his estate on the South coast by car.[1]

The Tchaer estate had been acquired as early as 1902 and consisted of approximately four hundred *desiatinas* of land situated on the very shore of the Black Sea. Stana had turned the estate into a veritable heaven on earth. It was famed for its park which contained a unique collection of roses (to this day many remember the passionate tango "In the Tchaer Park the roses blossomed…"). On their arrival, the married couple occupied the main house, whilst Boldarev the secretary, doctor Malama, Sergei and Yelena of Leuchtenberg, set up home in the so-called "children's house". Prince Nicholas Orlov lodged at a villa in the nearby Kharax estate which belonged to Grand Duke George Mikhailovich. Peter Nikolaevich and his family moved to his own Dülber estate, also becoming a close neighbour.[2]

At first sight, nothing had changed at Dülber, remembered Prince Roman. In the castle, thanks to the work of the estate's manager, Demidov, everything had been kept in perfect order. In the park the lush shrubs were in full bloom, the mighty cedars had scattered their crowns and, as ever, the shapely and proud cypresses stretched towards the blue sky. Eternal nature remained unperturbed by the tempests of political confusion. Soon Baron Stahl, the manager of the Znamenka estate near Peterhof, arrived from Petrograd with his family, and with unsettling news. He brought the entire accounts for all of Peter Nikolaevich's lands. Their financial condition was lamentably poor. Some of the estates had been caught in territories directly affected by military actions. Having literally been turned into battlefields, they had ceased to produce any income. Payments from the Department for Crown Lands had only been made for the first quarter of 1917 which amounted to a paltry sum. The Court departments had effectively been wound up. This forced the immediate sale of the Katameiz estate near Yalta, where for twenty years Peter's family had cultivated a fruit garden famed for its superlative peaches and apricots.[3]

In March 1917 the press followed the fate of the members of the House of Romanov in detail. The *Southern Gazette* reported:

Grand Duke Dmitry Pavlovich [exiled to the Caucasus, a region of military activity, for his part in the assassination of Rasputin - Z.B.] informed his father that on the 26th of March he intends to return to Petrograd. His departure has been delayed by the military encounters taking place on the border with Persia.

Despite the assertions of Petrograd's newspapers, the question of Marie Feodorovna's departure for Livadia has not yet been resolved. In order to resolve the question her Chamberlain, Prince Shervashidze has left for Petrograd on the instructions of Marie Feodorovna.

Anastasia and Militza Nikolaevny have left Kiev. It is rumoured that they are to join Nicholas Nikolaevich. Grand Duke Alexander Mikhailovich, having sent his request to be allowed to resign from his position as Inspector of the air force, is continuing to perform his duties in this post until his request is answered.

The Dowager Empress Marie Feodorovna has presented the Provisional Committee of the State Duma with a petition for the nomination of a commissar to escort her from Kiev to the Inkerman station on the Southern shore of the Crimea.[4]

Grand Duchess Xenia Alexandrovna informed Nicholas II in a letter of the 23rd of March, sent from Petrograd to Tsarskoe Selo:

I have been sitting here in the hope that they would let me through to you, as my one wish was to see you. Now it has become clear that it isn't feasible, and I leave for the Crimea on the 25th.

You will understand how painful and sad it is for me, but what can I do, I have to give up. With all my heart and soul

I remained with you through the illnesses of the dear children, in the times of fear, though far away, cut off without news, sharing your sufferings, and bearing your torments together with you. Today Mama, Sandro and Olga and her husband leave for the Crimea. They will be staying with us [in Ai Todor – Z.B.].

For poor Mama the return to the Crimea will be so painful, but we shall at least be all together, and that is such a consolation in our times! What a pity that you can't come and be with us! One only hopes that everything will end for the best for Russia, and that we shall win the war.

My heart cries bloody tears when I think of you, of our homeland, of everything. But God…will be merciful to Russia. Yes, with God's help we shall meet in better circumstances, but where, when, and how? [5]

On the 25th-26th of March 1917 the "Kiev" Romanovs reached the Crimea. The Dowager Empress, accompanied by her son-in-law and younger daughter, Grand Duchess Olga Alexandrovna and her morganatic husband, Captain Nikolai Kulikovsky, arrived at the Ai Todor estate owned by Grand Duke Alexander Mikhailovich (Sandro) and his wife. The Empress's lady-in-waiting, Countess Zinaida Mengen, and nurse Vasilieva, who worked in Kiev in the hospital of Grand Duchess Olga, accompanied them.

Olga and her husband settled at Kharax on their arrival. At that stage George Mikhailovich himself was living in Gatchina, from where he moved to Finland and tried, in vain, to get permission to leave for England. He wanted to be reunited with his wife and two daughters*, who were lucky enough to have left Russia before the beginning of the First World War.

There are two versions of events explaining the circumstances of Marie Feodorovna's departure from Petrograd for Kiev. It is possible that in the spring of 1916 she had a troubled

---

* George Mikhailovich (1863–1919), grandson of Emperor Nicholas I, third son of Grand Duke Mikhail Nikolaevich, was married to a Greek Princess, Grand Duchess Maria Georgievna (1876–1940), and had two daughters, Princess Nina (1901–1974) and Xenia (1903–1965).

conversation with her son, where the Empress-Mother demanded Rasputin's removal from Petrograd. If her demand were not met, she herself would leave. As always the Emperor washed his hands of the affair. He didn't wish to upset his wife: "better one Rasputin, than ten scandals a day."* The second version asserts that the Empress-Mother wished to be closer to the Headquarters in order to see her son more frequently.

> With the return of Marie Feodorovna from the Headquarters (9th of March 1917 – Z.B.) reigning silence in the Kiev Palace has only taken a firmer hold. There are almost no receptions, and the usual visits to the hospital have been halted. From the outside the palace maintains its former appearance. Previously the Tsarina's arrival in Kiev from Petrograd was explained by Marie Feodorovna's interference in the Rasputiniad. However, those close to the Tsarina-Mother categorically deny this version, although they believe that there is a connection between the Rasputiniad and the publication of Nicholas Mikhailovich's letter, which was written at Marie Feodorovna's request.[6]

Whatever the reason, on the 1st of May, 1916, Marie Feodorovna left the Anichkov Palace, her residence on Nevsky Prospekt in the capital, for Kiev, a fact which is confirmed by a note in the Palace daily journal. In the Emperor's diary entry for the 8th of May, 1916, his arrival in Kiev is noted with the words: "…to our joy we were met by dear Mama and Olga."[7]

The extent to which the life of Marie Feodorovna, an elderly woman approaching her seventies, had been disturbed can be judged by her correspondence with her daughter Xenia, her most trusted confidante and supporter. In the autumn and

---

* The Emperor's answer to Prime-Minister V.N.Kokovtsev on being presented with a document outlining Rasputin's shaming of the Tsar's family and dynasty (*Diaries*, p. 27).

towards the end of 1916, Xenia was forced to live in the Crimea, due to the illnesses of her children, and she often wrote to her mother in Kiev from Ai Todor. She returned to Petrograd on the eve of the revolution, on the 19th of February, 1917.

From Xenia to her Mother. Ai Todor.
28th of October, 1916.

Nicky arrived... **it seems that you haven't seen Nicky since May, which is six months!!** [author's emphasis — Z.B.].What would have happened if dear Papa were still alive? Would there have been war — disorder, intellectual ferment, dissents — in a word, everything that is happening, or not — I think not — at least <u>much of it</u> would not be taking place, and that we can say with certainty. There wouldn't be in R. [Russia — Z.B.] (for one thing!) all these surprise ministers, all this chaos! One simply cries out in despair, but alas! It's no use![8]

In October 1916, the fiftieth anniversary of the arrival in Russia of the highborn betrothed, the Danish Princess Dagmar, who would later become the Empress Marie Feodorovna, was celebrated with fitting ceremony. The Emperor came to the celebrations in Kiev, after a six-month separation from his mother. In his diary entry for the 28th of October we find:
"At 10.30 we arrived in Kiev. Dear Mama met us at the station. Went to the St. Sophia Cathedral with Alexei, and then on to the palace. Sat with Mama. The three of us breakfasted... After tea at Mama's returned to the train. At 8.15 dined with Mama and stayed with her until 11.30."[9]
As always, there are only facts in the Emperor's diary, no thoughts, and no emotions, even on such a jubilee occasion.

From Marie Feodorovna to Xenia, having heard of the murder of Rasputin and the ensuing repression of the participants in the conspiracy, including members of the Family:
4th of January, 1917.
(In a mixture of Russian, French and English words.)

I'm trying to keep a hold on myself, but it is <u>too</u> difficult. I think everybody is raving mad. The poor family wrote a <u>stupid</u> letter that was sent back to M.P.* with a dreadful inscription.

* Probably, Marie Pavlovna Sr., one of the initiators of the letter.

Such a toss in the face of them all. Poor A.Olga* having signed it too. They ought never to have done it, <u>ridiculous</u> style and why the whole family en bloc? So now they are all looked upon as having taken part in the... A. Miechen sent me the copy accompanied by a few words terribly offended and furious asking me to come back and help. As if there was a possibility for me to do it. Of course <u>if</u> I could help <u>him</u> out of it, I'd certainly go and try at once. For the moment two of the br's in law** are here, <u>very</u> fatiguing, as they quarrel the whole time and make one quite uncomfortable. Bimbo was perfectly out of his wits at first. But apropos it amuses him as a sport. He showed me N's letter <u>ordering</u> him to leave the capital for Grush (Grushevka — Z.B.) and now he remained quietly three days here without understanding that Kiev is not Grush! They are surrounded by detectives like real criminals. I feel very low and horrified, one does not know what is coming next. Where will it lead us! to the devil, I think, if God won't stop it.[10]

From Marie Feodorovna to Xenia.
Kiev. 11th of January, 1917.

In my thoughts I am always with you, and I am sorry that we didn't meet. Especially on this terrible time when all the bad passions seem to have taken possession of the capital. The hatred augments daily for her that is disastrous, but doesn't open eyes yet. One continues quietly to play with the fire. I hear she gets heaps of anonymous letters & even telegrams where they ask her not to listen what people say, but continues her work: 'dark forces and bright forces help you' and of course she believes them***... What my poor dear Nicky must suffer makes me mad to think! Just everything might have been so excellent after the <u>man's</u> disappearance and now it was all spoiled by her rage and fury, hatred and feeling of revenge!... so sad...[11]

* The Queen of the Hellenes, Grand Duchess Olga Constantinovna.
** Grand Dukes Nicholas (Bimbo) and George Mikhailovichi.
*** Sandro assured that these letters and telegrams were fabricated by Protopopov, Minister of Interior (letter to Xenia dated 09.01.1917, unpublished).

In Xenia's letter of the 21st of January 1917 the Family's indignation at Alexandra Feodorovna's meddling in state affairs can clearly be heard. She tells her mother that it is difficult for everyone, but

...for you it is a hundred times worse. Dear Mama, what can you do? If you speak you must and shall be listened to...if things don't change it will be the end of everything. People seem to have put their last hope in you and if that fails — it may only be fatal. If only he would return to Stavka and you could join him there and see him <u>alone</u>. But, as if on purpose, he doesn't return!"[12]

And again, from Ai Todor, from Xenia to her mother. 26th of January, 1917.

...then Mitya* came. He read me the famous letter from the family to Nicky out loud. I understand that it could have enraged him, and Mitya also thinks that it's difficult to imagine a more unfortunate move; the family should never have acted in this manner, and of course it can only have discredited itself in Nicky's eyes! He and Tatiana** live like accomplished hermits, never visit anyone, never see anyone. He (Mitya) suggested to go to Stavka when <u>she</u> is away, otherwise there's <u>no point, one can't argue with her</u>.[12]

The Empress-Mother's hostile attitude towards Alexandra is similarly visible in her letter of the 10th of February, 1917: "I wonder if she will forgive and humble herself at least." Vital information was passed on in the letter of the 21st of February 1917, from Xenia in Petersburg, to her mother: "Nicky...is at last leaving this afternoon for Stavka. Perhaps you can now travel to him and see him alone."[12] And, in fact, the Emperor did at last leave for the General Headquarters on the 22nd of February.

Olga Alexandrovna's diary entry on the 3rd of March 1917, bears witness to the shock that Marie Feodorovna experienced on hearing of her son's abdication: Sandro remembered that he

---

* Grand Duke Dmitry Constantinovich (1860–1919) who at that time stayed in his recently acquired estate, Kichkine (Tartar for "Baby").

** The daughter of KR, and widow of Prince Constantine Bagration-Mukhranski.

"had never seen the Empress Marie in such a condition, unable to sit calmly for a moment, endlessly pacing up and down the room. It was clear that she was angry rather than unhappy. She understood nothing of what had happened, but blamed everything on Alix."[13]

On the 9th of March, 1917, Marie Feodorovna returned to Kiev from Mogilev, where she saw her son for the last time, and immediately sent a letter to Xenia.

These times and conditions are so difficult and incomprehensible, that I don't understand <u>anything</u> anymore. I am only happy to be with poor Nicky, a true martyr! You can't imagine what happens to my soul and how I <u>suffer</u> to see him in this position! It's simply unbelievable![14]

From Marie Feodorovna to Xenia.
Kiev. 22nd of March, 1917.

...I still can't believe that this dreadful nightmare is real. I hear <u>nothing</u> from poor Nicky, for which I suffer <u>horribly</u>. Will she ever understand what she did? I am sure not, she is too proud and obstinate, what hell it must be! I'm even frightened to think of it! I am very sorry for my granddaughters, and little Marie is so ill! And I know nothing![15]

In Petrograd Xenia became an eyewitness of threatening revolutionary upheavals. Her diary entries for the 24th, 27th and 28th of February and from the 1st to the 11th of March are of immense value for historical research. An excerpt from this diary, dated 12th March 1917, with the specific characteristics of the original script preserved, will confirm this assertion:

...they told how in Pavlovsk, at night (at about 10), a crowd of soldiers and similar riff-raff with machine-guns rushed in, and they demanded that they be given arms. Mar. Nik Baulina met them and asked them to leave and not to make so much noise, so as not to scare "Her Majesty". "And who's Her Majesty?" — "The Queen of Greece". "We don't need any Greek Queen" and they left, but they robbed Elena P.* stealing her valuable

* The widowed Queen of Greece, Grand Duchess Olga Constantinovna, frequently stayed in Pavlovsk during the First World War, and she was there during the February revolution. Yelena Petrovna, Princess of Serbia, was the wife of the owner of Pavlovsk, Prince Ioann Constantinovich.

things which hadn't been put away (she was in P. [Petrograd]) and boots and warm clothes from the children — Terrible — what a disgrace. I am so tired I can't stand it!.. Sandro... telegraphed that he's intending to leave for Ai Todor... and to ask the government to hasten her [Marie Feodorovna's — Z.B.] departure — poor, poor Mama, still that trial... the Crimea! [16]

Xenia's correspondence with her mother during these days continued at a pace, and on the 14th of March the following letter was sent to Kiev:

...I am happy that you agreed to go to Ai Todor. To get away from everything and everyone and hide in a corner. In front of you I am ashamed of my country, yes, simply ashamed and embarrassed that everything crumbled so quickly and that nobody resisted or stood up for Nicky! Poor, unhappy man, what must he endure and think of his "loyal subjects"?! I am seized by rage at the thought of those who destroyed him... I travel by horse-driven cab, as all our cars have been taken...[17]

But the Romanovs' "cursed days" had only begun. In the unpredictable and horrifying first weeks of the revolution, the Crimea appeared to be a comparatively calm and safe haven, serenely remote from military or political conflict.

In his *Reminiscences*, Sandro writes that none of the Romanovs located in Kiev at this stage wished to leave. Personally, he would have preferred to remain closer to the front, even though all male members of the Family had been forced to resign their commissions. For these men, prepared from early childhood for careers in military service, enforced retirement was an almost unendurable torment. How could the days be filled, when all around there was instability, uncertainty and alarm? What of their families? Until the middle of March the streets in Kiev were filled with endless, unruly meetings, demonstrations, marches with flags and new political slogans demanding an immediate armistice, a return of husbands and sons from the front, and an independent Ukraine. For the time being the Romanovs were treated with calm and restraint.

Kiev suddenly became alien and dangerous, where all of a sudden they turned into "The Romanovs, enemies of the revolution and of the Russian people"[18]. The Dowager Empress suffered particularly. The day came when the gate of the hospital of which she was a patron was closed before her, and the head doctor directly announced, expressing the opinion of the medical staff, that her presence was undesirable. The gloomy parting with her son in Mogilev deepened the sense of uncertainty in regard to the future, and Nicky's fate, and the fate of the family in general. The lamentable silence of royal relatives in high places was little consolation: why were her nephew, the English King George V and her sister Queen Alexandra, taking so long? What was her other nephew in Copenhagen, King Christian X doing? What of the related royal families of Spain, Sweden, Greece and Rumania? And to add insult to injury, there were the hurtful jibes and nicknames being attached to their names and titles. "The Empress, verging on seventy years of age, couldn't comprehend and didn't want to believe that the dynasty that had given Russia Peter the Great, Alexander I, Alexander II, and finally her own husband Alexander III, who she worshipped, could be accused of hostility to the Russian people. Shaking from indignation, she couldn't be told when this horror would end. She didn't believe that her son or grandson would no longer be Emperor. On hearing of the Provisional Government and Soviets' intention to exile the Emperor to Siberia, she asserted her own intention to accompany him into exile in Siberia, as it appeared to her that again, as in Mogilev, during her son's departure from the army, he was in need of his mother's support."[19]

Within the last ten days of March a commissar came to the family and passed on a decree of the Provisional Government, ordering them to immediately leave for the Crimea. The Kiev Soviet approved this decision, and was happy to rid itself of these "enemies of the people", who had washed up so close to the front. "We practically had to carry the Empress to the station. She fought until the last few minutes, wishing to stay and declaring that she would prefer to be arrested and thrown in prison."[20] The Romanovs managed to leave and safely reached the Crimea in a convoy of sailors. The journey took four days. At every station crowds of refugees tried to force their way onto the train, but the bared bayonets of the escort repelled them. At the Sevastopol city station the family disembarked to procede and take up residence at Ai Todor, the palace owned by Sandro. There they were met by somebody with the immodest title of "Special Commissar of the Provisional Government" who immediately gave them a list of restrictions.

Grand Duchess Xenia at last managed, on the 25th of March, to leave Petrograd with her six sons, Sofia Dmitrievna Yevreinova, a lady-in-waiting, and her husband's adjutants, Prince Orbeliani, General Vogel and the head of the household, Chatelen. On the 28th of March, during Holy Week, she reached Ai Todor, and the whole family was finally together, albeit under unofficial house arrest. Although Sandro writes that they "could only move freely within the confines of the Ai Todor estate, on the fifteen or so *desiatinas* of land between the mountains and the shores of the sea", from the entries in Xenia's diary we get a slightly different picture of comparative freedom. In April and May mention is made of trips to Yalta to a notary, walks in Koreiz to the Yusupovs, and visits to the Vorontsov family in Alupka. They walked, gardened, fished, played tennis and went on picnics.

Apparently straight after her arrival on the 28th of March, Xenia writes in her diary: "Mama talked a lot about poor Nicky and their meeting and about entourage which hasn't now abandoned him and about Ruzsky who was rude with him and disgusting. I recounted what we had gone through in P. [Petrograd]... Mama was outraged that they hadn't let me see Nicky... Mama has caught herself wishing to go home to Livadia!"[22] The unfortunate woman hadn't understood that her beloved Livadia had been nationalised, and now had a new set of masters. We learn news of the new residents of the former imperial residence from a letter sent to the editor of the *Yalta Life* newspaper:

> I left Commissar Zadunovsky at his residence in the nationalised Livadia with a heavy feeling of offence and bitterness. It was here that I narrowly escaped being hit by a car travelling at high speed around Livadia, in which the artist Chaliapin and his family were sitting.[23]

It would appear that the sumptuous Tauride had remained unchanged, with its enchanting beauty: a wonderful, fairytale retreat on the very shores of the blue sea, the lush flowerings of the gardens, and the warmth of early summer. But there was little cause for rejoicing. From the newspapers they had learnt that the Tsar's family were under arrest in Tsarskoe Selo, and they were concerned as to their fate. It was hoped that they would be allowed to move abroad. From the North came unbelievable and contradictory snippets of information, the situation on the front-line was depressing, and there were rumours of the collapse of the army and the fleet. The behaviour of the local servants and retainers was another source of surprise and pain, as they became increasingly unruly and began to slowly slip away.

2/15 April. Xenia's diary.

> This morning we exchanged Easter greetings and kisses with the local retainers. A major scandal with the cook and the food's unrestrained theft. The cook has been called up into the army and is leaving and today he refused to cook, and left us without sugar and flour. Sofia Dm. and Vogel will start managing the household... Olga Orlova* is living in Dülber.[24]

What of the daily life of the relations and neighbours living in close proximity to Ai Todor? The coexistence was not simple.

"Uncle Nikolasha lived a cloistered life in his Tchaer and refused any travellers from the North, no matter who they were. I visited Aunty Stana and Uncle fairly frequently. He often went

---

* Born Belosselskaya-Belozerskaya, her married name was Princess Olga Constantinovna Orlova, the subject of V.A.Serov's famous portrait.

down to the shore with his hunting rifle to shoot... I also visited Nadya's father-in-law, Count Orlov, who was living apart from his wife at Kharax. During such visits I often met Uncle Sandro and his children on the lower street, crossing the path on their way from Ai Todor to the sea. I didn't really know my cousins very well. They mixed with the children of the Emperor, the Sheremetevs, and the Vorontsovs, and were friendly with them. If we met on the country road we would barely exchange a few words."[25]

The Romanovs, under unofficial arrest, were at first treated by the local population, particularly in Yalta, with sympathy and with the respect reserved for them in former times. The new powers attempted to arouse feelings of hostility and envy. Already in May of 1917, an article published in the *News of the Tavrichesky Regional Social Committee*, discussed the situation in Yalta:

> ...a fabulous place, a healing retreat, surrounded by former Tsarist estates and those of his kin. Special efforts were made and stringent measures undertaken to ensure that all those who settled here were "loyal", not through fear, but through their genuine devotion to the Tsar. Only monarchists were allowed to come here to live... for decades a process of "natural selection" of the population was enforced to guarantee peaceful rest for Nicholas. No surprise then, that he wished to settle at Livadia following his abdication, as he was convinced of the loyalty of the inhabitants of Yalta.
>
> ...With open discontent they endure the freeing of political prisoners, who are now living where formerly only the Father-Tsar was allowed to reside, and disguise their dissatisfaction with difficulty, calling them nothing other than "convicts", and pointing them out to one another like wild animals.

E.K.Breshko-Breshkovskaya [the Russian "Grand-mother" of the revolution – Z.B.] who resided at Livadia from the 1st to the 4th of June they dubbed a "yid". The local government has been besieged by complaints of disrespect to the former Tsarist estates. "The common public now stroll in Livadia and Massandra, taking walks and pulling up flowers, often driving through, kicking up dust and disturbing us," 'citizens' complain. Those who are now arriving in Yalta, are the people who could not approach at a stone's throw.[26]

Life on the three estates continued, for better or for worse. The commissar was a representative of the Provisional Government, whilst the sailors were subordinated to the local Soviet, providing a perfect example of divided (dual) authority at a low level. The cynical sailors had the upper hand however, and they didn't attempt to conceal their contempt for the commissar: they failed to fulfil his commands, and even refused to stand up when he arrived, underlining their lack of respect. The Romanov's ability to ignore their custodians, and their ability to give the impression that they weren't even aware of their existence, infuriated the guards and drove them on to further extremes of uncouthness and cynicism. Empress Marie sat from morning to evening on the veranda engrossed in reading the old family Bible, with which she, as a highborn betrothed, had arrived in Russia from her native Copenhagen, and which she always took with her on her travels. The greatest difficulty for her was to understand why everyone was cramping in together at Ai Todor.

"Our commissar had a frightened, bitter expression which never left his face. He was forever taking peeks at his assistants, who terrorized him, and in his dealings with us he attempted to copy their revolutionary abruptness. In April he entitled me the 'former Grand Duke Alexander', and in June I have transformed into 'Admiral Romanov'. Towards June

I have already become simply 'citizen Romanov'. Any attempt at protest would have made him a happy man."[27]

And yet one can be struck by the omnipotent love happenings, when amongst the imprisoned Romanovs several weddings were celebrated. From Xenia's diary from the 12th (25th) of April:

> This afternoon Mama and all of us went to Kharax and watched Nadya and Vl. Orlov's* wedding from afar [the bridegroom was Nicholas Orlov — Z.B.]. Wladi Orlov was in a vast white Circassian coat. Nikolasha and Petiusha** were also in Circassian coats. Seriozha Leucht***: in civvies with a red tie. We couldn't see the bride properly, but Marina was in a fantastic nurse's dress. We returned for tea and discussed our impressions a great deal. We weren't invited, as they feared a family assembly and everything was in strict incognito.[28]

The same event is described in the reminiscences of Prince Roman: on the 10th of April Nadezhda (Nadya), the daughter of Grand Duke Peter was married to Prince Nicholas Orlov. The parents of the young couple decided to celebrate the event in a close family circle, due to the political situation in Russia, and in order not to overly attract the attention of the local population. They didn't even invite the Empress-Mother and the other relatives from Ai Todor. The marriage took place in the tiny St.Nina's Church, built at Kharax in the Georgian style, according to Grand Duke George Mikhailovich's wishes. The bridegroom's best men were Sergei Leuchtenberg, Count Stefan Tyshkevich and Roman Petrovich. There were about fifteen or sixteen close relatives in all. On leaving the church Roman noticed something rustling in the bushes. In fact Sandro was hiding there and observing the ceremony with his sons. After the wedding the newlyweds settled in Yalta.[29]

* Prince Nicholas Orlov, son of Olga Constantinovna and Vladimir (Wladi) Orlov.
** The family names for Nicholas and Peter Nikolaevichi.
*** Duke Sergei Georgievich of Leuchtenberg, son of Stana by her first marriage.

Almost within a week another marriage was celebrated, between Yelena of Leuchtenberg and Count Stefan Tyshkevich, a Horse-Guards officer. There were two services, as the Count was a Catholic. The Catholic service took place at the Church of Miskhor. The second, in the Russian Orthodox rite, took place at the same little church at Kharax where Nadya had only just been married.

By the 16th/29th of April, Xenia is already entering her diary with alarm:

…They say that in Sevastopol the disorder amongst the sailors is terrible and Kolchak* is totally in the hands of the sailors. Nobody has any civic fortitude. Very sad… Changes in the uniforms of the fleet, and the central part of a cockade is now coloured in red. They have renamed all the craft that formerly carried the names of emperors: Alexander III — *Freedom*, Paul I — *The Republic*, Nicholas I — *Democracy*, Catherine II — *Free Russia*.[30]

Within a few weeks the situation for the inhabitants of Dülber, Tchaer and Ai Todor had considerably worsened. At a meeting of the regional committee, on the 14th of April, a resolution was passed on the question of *The Romanovs and former dignitaries*:

The question has been raised, and a concern expressed, that the presence of such a large number of such individuals in one place is not desirable. In the interests of safety they should be resettled separately at different ends of the empire and not given the opportunity to disseminate harmful propaganda. The proposal was met with loud applause.[31]

The Sevastopol Soviet believed that the Romanovs in the Crimea could stand at the head of a counter-revolutionary

* As a result of the total anarchy in the Navy the sailors disarmed their officers and even demanded that their Admiral give in his personal weapon. Kolchak preferred to throw it overboard.

movement in the South of Russia. Its political authority already waning, the Provisional Government couldn't disregard the growth in influence of the Soviets over the mass of the semi-illiterate population. As a result, a search of the three estates was ordered, and took place on the night of the 26th of April 1917. The details of the search have been recorded in the memoirs of several members of the Family.

As Sandro recollects, "the search of the 26th was carried out by a crowd of sailors, armed to the teeth, who broke into the villa at about 4 o'clock in the morning, at daybreak. About fifty sailors arrived, as well as three trucks with soldiers and machine-guns. They wished to look in the large writing table in the library ('Give us the key. We're not going to break your furniture. It's all the property of the people.'). The ringleader seized a bundle of letters with foreign postage stamps, which had been received from English and French relatives ('Correspondence with the enemy... Not bad for starters!'), and then got to the letters written in Russian ('Correspondence with the former Tsar – a conspiracy against the revolution!'). They had come to seize any arms, and searched for machine-guns.

"Only at six o'clock in the evening did these people start back for Sevastopol, leaving the house in total disarray and taking my personal correspondence and the Bible which belonged to my mother-in-law. The Dowager Empress begged them not to deprive her of that valuable, and offered all her jewels in return for it.

'We're not thieves,' the leader of their gang proudly announced, terribly disappointed by the failure of his mission. 'This is a counter-revolutionary book, and such a respected lady as yourself shouldn't poison her mind with such rubbish'.

"Ten years later, already in Copenhagen, my aged mother-in-law received a package containing her Bible. A Danish diplomat bought the Bible from a Moscow bookstore dealing in rare publications. Empress Marie died with that book in her hands."[32]

The nightmare of that April night is reflected in Xenia's diary:

At half past five we were awoken by a frenzied banging on the door... and a loud, foul voice "open this door immediately... Immediately! (Sandro opened)... a monster in the uniform of a volunteer... who announced that "in the name of the Provisional Government and the Soviet of Workers and Soldiers' Deputies I arrest you all, and there will now be a search." At the same time another sailor came in through another door with a rifle. The volunteer said: "I would ask you Duchess to put your hands on top of the blanket," to which Sandro asked: "Do you really think she's armed?" [A description of the search of the bed follows, whereby the pillows were turned inside out, and the cupboards, boxes etc. were searched.] [33]

Here is Roman's description of the search at Dülber:

"On the night of the 26th of April, 1917, I was woken by the door into my bedroom being opened. I turned the light on and saw a sailor with a gun. Behind him I noticed someone who was strangely dressed, lighting up the walls of the room with a hand-held torch. This person, who had a red band on his sleeve, ordered me to remain in bed while he searched my two rooms. The sailor with the gun stood guard next to my bed. Whilst I was lying still, I couldn't help thinking of my parents and Marina, who were no doubt enduring a similar search. The man with the red band, a commissar from the Soviet, began ransacking the room. He poked his nose into all the corners, went through the books, opened my writing desk, from which he took letters, papers, documents and a notebook. Everything that he took he stuffed into an enormous case. Passing by me to search the second room, he ordered me to get dressed, but not to leave the building until the search was completed." In the absence of the commissar Roman spoke with the sailor who had only just been called up into the fleet and expressed a hatred of the deputies of the Soviet. The search of the entire house was completed, and Roman hurried to his parents. The same man with the red band was searching all their rooms and took a pile of papers from Stana's writing desk, in which she had spent years writing the names and types of flowers to be grown in the garden. "The notes also contained the names of firms, Russian, French, and German, where mother placed her orders. No doubt these addresses were of immense importance to those who were seeking the plans of counterrevolutionaries!"[34]

Marina's letters and Gospels were taken from her room. All the servants of the house were also searched. Two revolvers, belonging to Roman and his father, for which they had the necessary permits, were seized along with the hunting rifles. The commissar took all "suspicious" documents and letters. After this night visitation by a large number of sailors, it was discovered that several silver knives and forks had gone missing, as well as a ring belonging to one of the maids.

On the same night a search was carried out at Tchaer. The commissar of the Provisional Government, Senior Lieutenant Verkhovsky, arrived. The valet woke Nikolasha. Verkhovsky introduced himself and showed his order for the search, signed by the commander of the Black Sea Fleet, Rear-Admiral Lukin, and a telegram from the Provisional Government. Signed by A.Kerensky and Prince Lvov, the telegram ordered that the members of the Family be rehoused in a maximum of two estates, and that those returning from the front should not be allowed to reach the arrested individuals. All forms of motor transport should be confiscated; all forms of written correspondence should be kept under strict control, and all servants or staff of foreign descent or prisoners of war should be removed [Both documents are kept by descendants abroad. – Z.B]. During the search the Grand Duke's revolver and hunting rifles were seized, as were Stana's letters, and an exercise book containing Boldarev's poetry. Verkhovsky literally emptied the drawers of Nikolasha's desk, though he failed to capture any documents of a political or military nature, as they were located in a suitcase, which the commissar didn't notice.[35]

In response to the search of the three estates Sandro wrote a letter of protest and sent it to the Provisional Government. The letter was taken by Felix Yusupov directly to Kerensky with a notification that many of the Romanovs' valuables had gone missing, and a demand for an explanation as to what right the search had to take place.

Within two days, by the order of the Provisional Government, a special military unit appeared, and watch was kept on the strip of seashore. At the entrance to the estates guardposts were set up, and soldiers regularly patrolled the gardens and parks. The small house, which was formerly inhabited by the gardeners and park keeper, was transformed into a barrack.

An official explanation of the search was printed in the *News of the Tavrichesky Regional Social Committee* on the 30th of April 1917, under the headline "The Search of the members of the family of the former Tsar and their retainers in Yalta":

> The following telegram was sent to Petrograd, to Minister Kerensky: "In response to your telegram No.4689 the Commander instructed Lieutenant-Colonel Verkhovsky by Order No.5771 and the Sevastopol Central Committee to take measures to prevent possible counter-revolutionary propaganda. The existence of such activities can be presupposed due to the host of rumours gathered by the specially assigned member of the Central Committee, which told of night meetings, of trusted individuals being sent to the fronts, of correspondences, of radio-transmitters, of secret automobiles running at fixed times at night.
>
> In order to check this received material, and obtain concrete information on the situation, as well as to calm the seriously alarmed public opinion, specially appointed members of the Sevastopol Central Committee, Lieutenant-Colonel Verkhovsky and the Commissar for Yalta, Priselkov, have adopted the plan of a sudden search of all individuals who were subject to certain suspicions…

Ливадія. Большой дворецъ.   Крымъ — Crimée.
Livadia. Grand Palais.

The old Livadia Palace,
where Emperor
Alexander III died
in 1894.
Before 1910

Nikolasha
and his wife Stana
in the rose garden
at Tchaer estate.
Before 1917

Kharax in 1995, a sanatorium at present,
photographed by Author

Dülber estate in 1995, a sanatorium at present,
photographed by Author

Ruins of St. Nina's Church near Kharax in 1995,
photographed by Author

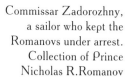

Commissar Zadorozhny,
a sailor who kept the
Romanovs under arrest.
Collection of Prince
Nicholas R.Romanov

At Dülber under arrest.
Collection of Prince Nicholas R. Romanov

Participants of
the theatrical performance in Dülber. 1918.
Collection of Prince M. Romanov

Empress Marie Feodorovna
aboard H.M.S.
Malborough. 1919.
The Romanovs album

H.M.S.
Malborough.
1919

Grand Duke Nicholas
(Nikolasha) wearing
his famous Circassian coat

Grand Dukes
Nicholas
and Peter with
their families
before sailing
off from
Constantinople.
1919.
Courtesy of
Princess
Jean Galitzine.
London

A letter of Empress Marie Feodorovna,
often in mixed languages

Grand Duchess Xenia Alexandrovna, her children
and her daughter-in-law, from the Romanovs album

The family of Grand Duke Peter
in emigration: his daughter Marina,
his son Roman and his daughter-in-law
Praskovia (née Countess Sheremetev).
Prince Nicholas Romanov collection

In order to maintain the secrecy and suddenness of the search, only a very limited number of persons were warned. The telephone and telegram exchanges were occupied by the armed forces. The members of the investigation committee, the troops and sailors, having arrived on *King Charles* and *Denmark* transports by night, immediately began work. All the searches took place simultaneously at daybreak on the 26th of April, and continued until three or four p.m. Members of the Sevastopol Central Committee conducted the search. In almost every group there was a worker, an officer, a soldier, a sailor, a counter-intelligence agent, experienced in search procedure, and members of the Professional Women's Union, for the searching of ladies. Each group had a responsible leader, equipped with written mandates. A large amount of papers and correspondences was detected and passed on to the investigation commission of the Sevastopol Committee. In view of the fact that during the search no direct proof of counter-revolutionary organizations was found, none of the named individuals were arrested. In order to control entry and exit from the estates of the members of the former Tsar's family, the Tchaer, Dülber and Ai Todor estates were put under a military guard made up of special detachments, which will prevent any contact with servicemen from the front.

Information on the replacement of the commandant, the concentration of the members of the former Tsar's family in one district, the requisition of automobiles, the removal of prisoners of war from the estates, and other measures undertaken, will be passed on in a detailed report..."[36]

By an order of the Provisional Government a commission was set up to look into Sandro's protest. The commission began by visiting Ai Todor to listen to the complaints. In Dülber the commission, chaired by Rear-Admiral Lukin, listened to the grievances of Nikolasha and Peter. Nikolasha's wrath was only restrained with difficulty by his brother. The commission returned the confiscated letters, notes and notebooks to Roman.

Formally the Romanovs were not yet under arrest. For the first few months of summer they could leave their estates. Roman frequently rode in a carriage to Yalta, met with Nadya's family and old friends, and played tennis. Militza walked in the park, and often called the old gardener over, in order to consult with him as to what and where to plant the next autumn. What optimism! Grand Duke Peter spent part of the day in his study drawing and planning buildings and churches, and he preferred not to discuss the events of the last few months. Marina painted. Roman walked in the park, talked with the soldiers, the majority of whom were friendly and affable. The press showed an interest in their daily life, and an article appeared under the headline "How the Romanovs Live in the Crimea":

It is well known that at present, at the Ai Todor estate, nine versts from Yalta, there are living: the mother of Nicholas II, Marie Feodorovna, her daughter Olga Alexandrovna Kulikovskaya with her sick husband Captain Kulikovsky and the former Grand Duke Alexander Mikhailovich with his wife, Xenia Alexandrovna, and their children.

Recently, Marie Feodorovna and Olga Alexandrovna, with the permission of the local authorities, visited Livadia. Escorted by the commissar's assistant and military delegates, Marie Feodorovna and her daughter visited the new Livadia Palace and the Livadia Park. A crowd of curious onlookers and soldiers from the local garrison gathered, and answered Marie Feodorovna's greeting with a deathly silence.

At Ai Todor Marie Feodorovna has begun occupying herself with horticultural pursuits. She zealously tends to her personal garden where she is cultivating asparagus.

Alexander Mikhailovich occupies himself with astronomy and vine-growing. At present he is introducing his children to physical labour, and together with them he is preparing firewood for the winter.

The former Supreme Commander of the Armed Forces Nicholas Nikolaevich lives at his spouse's estate, Tchaer (near Yalta). He leads a cloistered form of life, never venturing out, not even into the garden of his estate. Nicholas Nikolaevich spends most of his time writing his memoirs (reminiscences), which, in the opinion of informed individuals, are of great historical interest.

Apart from his memoirs, Nicholas Nikolaevich is at present writing an extensive history of the reign of Tsar Nicholas II, as well as finishing his article "Who is the Real Culprit of the World War", in which documents and figures of unique historical value will be presented, shedding light on the original cause of the conflict in Europe.

With the introduction of strict surveillance and control, the members of the former dynasty are totally deprived of freedom of movement. Their automobiles have been requisitioned. For the Romanovs' walks a so-called "neutral" zone (strip) has been arranged. On the outskirts of this strip patrol posts have been set up.

Correspondence, addressed to members of the former dynasty, which is voluminous and from every corner of Russia, is thoroughly checked by a special censor, and for the most part destroyed. In essence, almost all the letters addressed to the Romanovs are pleas and requests for material assistance.

Goods and produce for the members of the former dynasty are distributed by a rationing system, providing conditions equal to those for the general public, and none of the requests for extra food products are met. For example, Marie Feodorovna's request for three extra poods [1 pood = 16kg] of sugar for jam-making was refused.[37]

Nikolasha's memoirs were the grounds for a separate article, promising their publication in the near future*.[38]

In the newspapers, with increasing frequency, articles appeared on the Romanovs, which attempted to create a negative "public opinion" of their subjects. The authors of the articles insisted that only Alexander II had been popular with the local population, particularly amongst the Tartars. The Tsar would walk freely without an escort or retinue, and took part in hunts for mountain goats, for which the Tartars especially equipped themselves as beaters; whilst hunting the Tsar was on familiar terms with them and generously rewarded them. One expert on the mountains, a talented hunter and horseman, equipped himself with a special colourful outfit, decorated with silver and gold ribbons. Thus the profession of hunter-guide and a special livery appeared in the Crimea.

Alexander III was less popular amongst the inhabitants of the Southern shores:

His harsh temper was known to all, as was his irascibility, his predilection for parade-ground abuse and ruling with a fist,

* The aim of preparing the memoirs for print is to explore the attempts made by the central empires to conclude a separate peace with Russia at the expense of Siberia and the colonial possessions of France. Questions of internal politics in the memoirs are dealt with in depth, but this section will only be published after the death, not only of the Grand Duke, but of a number of dignitaries of the former ruling house.

which inclined people to keep at a safe distance. The Tartars couldn't forgive him his alcoholism. After the death of Alexander III a Tartar elder was heard to ask: "What sort of a Tsar was he? How could he control Russia if he couldn't even control himself? Is it even possible to imagine that every day a Tsar could drink himself into a stupor towards evening?"

As it happens, I heard from one of the Yalta doctors who took part in the autopsy and embalming of the body that alcohol had caused a horrifying devastation of Alexander III's organism. The organs had been destroyed. A minor case of influenza was enough to send this man, who only looked as if he was in the pink of good health, to the grave. During the post-mortem it was discovered that the heart had degenerated, that the kidneys were ruined, and the liver was a lump of material which had come unravelled.[39]

Further on the author of the article, M.Pervukhin, asserted that Nicholas II's popularity was negative. From many of the servants at Livadia he had personally "heard the opinion that from childhood the emperor was secretive and insidious. What he was thinking, only Alexandra knew. In contrast to his father, the last emperor was distinguished by his self-possession; he was always imperturbable, well brought up, polite, delicate. Affection shown towards his servants or officials signalled their dismissal from service the following day, a successor already having been found."[40]

There can be little doubt that articles of this type stirred up discontent, as towards the end of the summer the situation in the Crimea deteriorated significantly. Within the Black Sea Fleet the anti-officer mood strengthened, as did the wish not to take part in dangerous military operations. Deputation from the Baltic Fleet appeared in Sevastopol, representing the "Kronstadt Republic". "They looked unruly, with ragged hair, their caps set at a slant across their brows, and for some reason they all wore dark glasses... they moved into the good hotels and spent a lot of money."[41] The meetings were followed by open mutinies, where sailors disarmed their officers. Passions and disillusionment reached new heights when rumours spread telling of the collapse of the Russian offensive in Galicia, the counter-attack by the Austrians in July of 1917, and tales of mass desertion. In Petrograd there were calls for the overthrow of the Provisional Government which was fast losing its influence. Kerensky limited himself to giving fiery speeches at workers' meetings and at the front. In the summer of 1917 the Bolsheviks stood at the head of the revolutionary movement, whilst the Soviets confirmed their positions in the provinces. In Yalta a local Council of Deputies formed itself from workers, peasants and soldiers who began to control the police and search for counter-revolutionaries.

The Romanovs were forbidden to leave the territories of their estates. Only doctor Malama received permission to visit Dülber and Ai Todor in order to care for the sick. Thanks to Malama contact was kept with Yalta. "That's how we heard that our wonderful dentist from Yalta, Kostritsky, despite the risks, had journeyed to distant Siberia in order to give medical treatment to the Imperial family. Sergei Sergeievich was the court dentist, and he was often sent for when the Tsar's family was visiting Livadia. Returning from Tobolsk, he secretly brought letters for the Empress-Mother and Xenia."[42]

The most devastating news was that the Tsar's family had been sent not to the Crimea, as had been hoped, but to Siberia. Marie Feodorovna, having received a telegram informing her of their transfer to Tobolsk, suffered from a serious nervous shock and was confined to her bed for a lengthy period. An article appeared in the local press entitled *On the Illness of the Former Empress*:

> After the 3d-5th of July the question was raised in governmental circles of allowing

the Dowager Empress, as someone that has always kept out of political activity, to leave the boundaries of Russia on condition that she submits to all the demands of the government concerning the future of the Romanovs. However, Marie Feodorovna, for personal reasons didn't find it convenient to leave Russia until the end of the war, in particular as permission would only be granted in the event of her leaving for England or France, but not to a neutral state, for which the friends of the Empress were petitioning.

Intimates note that Marie Feodorovna has been unable to cope with the shock of the revolution. Formerly cheerful, despite her old age, in her letters from Ai Todor Marie Feodorovna continually recalls death, and asks for flowers to be left at Alexadner III's grave.[43]

In September the Empress's illness grew more severe. She didn't leave her bed, and her daughters and Sandro were permanently by her side. The British embassy was kept informed of her condition. It is possible that the term "friends of the Empress" included certain related royal Houses, who from the autumn of 1917 made attempts to move Minnie and her family out of the Crimea through the Balkan states. The Danish royal family and government became more active, giving their consent to the arrival of the Dowager Empress: on the 10th of September an encoded telegram was sent to the Danish embassy in Petrograd with an order to prepare for this event in the strictest secrecy. The Spanish King, Alfonso XIII attempted to find support in London and to come to an agreement with the Provisional Government on the ways for the departure of the Tsar and other Romanovs through Finland and Sweden.[44] As we know, these attempts were unsuccessful.

The encouragement of an atmosphere of hostility and envy, and a desire for revenge and a settling of accounts with the Tsar's family continued. The topic of the "Romanovs in the Crimea" didn't leave the pages of the newspapers. The Romanovs were accused of having bought up the finest lands on the coast from Tartar owners at pitifully low prices. Already at the beginning of the century, "to the advantage of one of the grand dukes, who was unhappy about the proximity to his fabulous estate of a noisy, dusty, dirty and poor Tartar village, located between Yalta and Alupka, the grand-ducal administration of the estate put pressure upon the peasants and obtained a verdict from the village assembly on the sale of the land to the grand duke, literally for a pittance. It is said that amongst crows, there are even white crows. But one honest eccentric was indeed found in the Crimean administration of that time... he refused to approve the verdict, having discovered that amongst the signatures to the verdict could be found the signatures of many who had long since passed away, moved to Turkey, been exiled to Siberia, or were under-age. The scandal was quickly covered up, the grand duke raised the price slightly, and the Tartar village was sent packing."[45]

The Romanovs were accused of a glaring infringement of one of the basic laws of the empire, in that they had not left the obligatory standardized strip of land bordering on the sea, that by law should have been open to common use. The stretch of land along the coast at Livadia was the first to be taken out of common use, followed by the land around Oreanda, and the rest soon followed. In effect nobody could use the coast and the neighbouring stretches of land, and fishermen didn't dare to near the shore, which was disastrous for their profession. (Probably the tradition of annexing these seashore belts for managerial and private residences, as was common practice under Stalin and the subsequent soviet bosses did not come out of the blue.)

The Romanovs had resisted the intrusion of the railroad on the Southern Coast.

The deceased writer Garin (the engineer Mikhailovsky) did surveying work for the construction of the Southern Coast railway on the eve of the Russo-Japanese war. According to his estimates the cost of the 200-verst railway track from Sevastopol to Feodosia would be one hundred million roubles, but it would increase the value of the territories served by a billion. The Romanovs didn't want the line to cut through their estates. The first project had to be reworked, this time going round the royal estates, increasing the cost of the works and lowering the significance of the economic benefits. Nicholas was already prepared to accept a concession when Grand Duchess Xenia, who had an immense influence on the Tsar, protested. She categorically announced that if the whistle of a locomotive was to be heard once in the Crimea, it would forever destroy the poetry of the Crimea, and she would immediately leave Russia for good.[45]

The press was insistent on the fact that anti-Semitism had been growing amongst the Romanovs since the times of Nicholas I. Until Alexander II the Southern Coast of the Crimea hadn't had the Pale of Settlement, the restricted areas where Jews were confined. Making use of the Tartars' idleness and the ignorance of the Greeks, the Jews had begun trading, opened shops, hotels, furnished rooms, set up a postal communication system, and provided all with a range of necessities. Under Alexander III hundreds of Jewish families had been removed from Yalta and Alupka as "harmful elements". Only those who had managed to register themselves amongst the local petty bourgeois or as merchants were allowed to stay. The situation verged on the absurd:

...The local authorities concluded a contract with the orchestra of the Preobrazhensky regiment, famed throughout Russia, but they were deprived of the right to perform in the Yalta civic gardens, as there were too many Jews amongst the musicians. In vain, attempts were made to receive a special permission, but it was not forthcoming. When the police evicted the widow of a local Jewish doctor she personally gave a plea to Nicholas II. Nicholas himself made a note on the plea: "There are too many Yids here as it is."[46]

...With long delays the postal system passed on rare letters from Siberia, from the arrested family of the Tsar. Particularly noteworthy are excerpts from the previously unpublished letters of Nicholas II that have been preserved abroad.

From Nicholas II to Xenia. Tobolsk.
23rd of September 1917.

...I recently received your letter from the capital of the 23rd of March,— written exactly six months ago... I also hoped that you would be able to visit us before going to the Crimea! And how **we** hoped that they would send us there and lock us up in Livadia — it would have at least been closer to you. How many times I asked Kerensky about that!

I saw Misha on the 31st of July in the evening; he looked well. And now he too is under arrest, poor thing, though I hope it won't be for too long!

...Studies with the children are slowly settling down just as in Tsarskoe Selo...

From Nicholas II to his mother. Tobolsk.
27th of October, 1917.

...I saw up a lot of firewood, usually with Tatishchev. Today I dug four holes with the riflemen for the posts to go under a new shed for winter firewood. One of them complimented me, as instead of two holes, with me he had dug four! The food here is excellent and in an abundance, unlike in Tsarskoe Selo, so we have put on a lot of weight, and gained 8—10 pounds...It's pleasant to reread Olga's letters — they breathe such happiness! Are you happy with Tikhon, your new grandson? To judge by her descriptions he's a wonderful, healthy little boy. God knows when we'll make his acquaintance?

...I read a lot. I've decided to read all our best writers from beginning to end! (I also read English and French books). I am studying Russian history with Alexei, which I love, and one could say, I know. The children's other studies are with Alix, M. Gilliard, Mr Gibbs, E.A.Schneider...[47]

Tobolsk. 10th of December, 1917.

My dear sweet Mama,

I just received Your sweet, priceless letter. I can't find the words to express to You all my joy and gratitude for it.

Xenia and Olga wrote and told me that You were intending to send me a letter; and I waited for it with trepidation and impatience — and at last it's arrived!!! I haven't written to You since the 27th of October, as I was worried that due to various events in Russia the post would be stopped. Luckily the post is working excellently, even in an exemplary fashion for such difficult times!

Only later did I read in the newspapers of the "search", which was in essence despicable theft, in your rooms in Ai Todor and only now do I understand the horror You must have suffered then! Diaries, letters, things etc. — what filth and baseness! Kerensky promised me that he would harshly punish the culprits and return everything to You that had been taken.

So many other people are in the same position. Of the more serious events I simply can not write, as they are too shameful and horrible!

...With the increasing heavy frosts it has become colder in the house, but not in all the rooms. In the hall, in girls' rooms and in my office it can be 9–10 degrees, but we dress warmly and it's perfectly bearable. We heat the house a great deal. Almost every day, after a walk, we have rehearsals of several plays (French). The first performance was on the 6th of Dec; Maria, Alexei and M.Gilliard* took part in it. It went very successfully — without a hitch!

In the full-length play, "Les deux timides", Tatiana, Anastasia, Valya D., M.Gilliard and I will act. It would probably be performed at Christmas. Another two are being prepared — English and French with different participants. The children's lessons of course are continuing ardently; as is my reading the rest of the time. And so the days and weeks fly by very quickly.

---

* M.Gilliard was at the court for thirteen years in his capacity as the tutor of the Tsar's children and followed them to Siberia as the former tutor of the heir to the throne, Tsesarevich Alexei.

How I would like to see You, my dear Mama, live near You, and share the suffering with You! We also haven't lost the hope, for one moment, that when all's said and done, the Merciful Lord will arrange everything for the better, for the best! It can't be that all the woes, all the horrors and violence, that have occurred in Russia have been for nothing, that is to say that they haven't brought some use, relief, renewal!

I hope that my letter will get to You towards Christmas (....), our prayers and thoughts will be particularly intimate and passionate in comparison with previous years! Alix, the children and I tenderly embrace You, dear Mama. God give you health and spiritual peace. — Kiss Xenia and Olga and best regards to all yours!

Christ be with You! Yours, limitlessly loving You,

Nicky.[48]

In the autumn of 1917 the army and fleet effectively ceased to exist as anarchy, mass desertion and crime ruled. The fall of the Provisional Government, expected from day to day, took place on the 26th of October, and the Romanovs' prison guards were immediately replaced.

On the 27th of October, instead of the "frightened, bitter commissar" of the Provisional Government, commissar Zadorozhny appeared, a taciturn sailor from the Black Sea Fleet, of unusually high stature for a sailor, in a leather coat and a cap pulled hard down over his forehead. He was a representative of the Sevastopol Soviet, the new power, who had this time been commanded to defend the Romanovs by a special order of Comrade Lenin himself, from attempts by the Yalta comrades to shoot the family right away. By a lucky coincidence, in 1916 Zadorozhny had served in the aviation school of Grand Duke Alexander Mikhailovich, which somewhat eased the relations with the new commissar.

From the first day of Zadorozhny's appearance the inhabitants of Tchaer, Ai Todor and Dülber found themselves under strict house arrest. Leaving the boundaries of the estates was categorically forbidden. The sailor appeared in the main building, handed out the post, which he had already opened and read, and arranged for the cook, Gromov, to prepare food for the guards. In a letter to Nicholas II from Ai Todor, dated the 30th of November 1917, Xenia informed her brother of the complete isolation from the outside world which had already been in effect for over a month. No coming in, nor going out, "we are boiling in our own juices".

From Xenia to Nicholas.
6th of December 1917.

...We continue to receive terrible news about our estates — they're taking everything, you can't say a word, and soon we'll be quite destitute. We've begun to wonder how we'll go on living, and how we'll earn our bread.

We have decided to open a hotel and have already allocated the positions: Sandro — Manager, Seriozha D. — doorman, Soph. Dm. — housekeeper, me — housemaid, Andrusha — chauffeur, Vogel — cashier, the younger boys — lift-boys, and so on.

Mama has a cold. For a month already we have heard nothing of Misha. He's been arrested again and set to P., but it seems that he's already returned.

Everything's so sordid, cruel and painful. It would be better to inflict it all on the Germans, rather than on our own people.[49]

Zadorozhny gave an order for all to move to Dülber, which could be more easily defended in the event of an attack by the Yalta comrades or an attempt to seize the Romanovs through force. In February 1918 the Empress Marie was transferred to Dülber, as were Sandro and his family and a few of their servants. Nadezhda Petrovna, having married N.Orlov, and Olga, the wife of Kulikovsky, were no longer considered to be Romanovs and were therefore not transferred.

Militza gave Minnie the best room with a view onto the sea and the Ai-Petri mountain peak. Both sisters, Militza and Stana, had deep feelings of gratitude and love for Marie Feodorovna. It is believed that Emperor Alexander III proposed that the Princesses of Montenegro be sent to Petersburg on reaching twelve years of age, to be educated at the Smolny Institute for aristocratic girls, under the personal patronage and supervision of the Empress Marie. They developed into brilliantly educated, well-read princesses, with a fluent command of several languages. During family meals at Aunty Minnie's, at the Anichkov Palace, where the Montenegrian girls would sit next to the Tsar's children and the young grand dukes, Peter Nikolaevich got to know his future bride. In 1889 he married Militza Nikolaevna, to the delight of Alexander III, who approved the choice of an Orthodox bride. The bride was dressed according to a ritual, which dated back one hundred and fifty years, and Empress Anna Ioannovna's diamond tiara was fixed in place on the bride's head by Marie Feodorovna herself.

Both sisters married at the same time, in 1889, Militza, as has been mentioned, to Grand Duke Peter, and Stana to Prince George Maximilianovich Romanovsky (de Beauharnais), the sixth Duke of Leuchtenberg (1852–1912), and at that time a widower with a seven-year old son, Alexander, by his first marriage. Both wedding ceremonies took place in Peterhof, with the gracious and generous participation of the Empress. Now, as their benefactress endured the most cruel testing of times, Militza and Stana tried to give her every possible attention.

At Minnie's and Xenia's suggestion the entire household dined together in the large dining room. At first the menu was very reasonable, if somewhat monotonous. But soon the portions had to be informally rationed and adjusted, and in the last weeks of arrest the meals became an unbroken chain of porridge, mildewed potatoes and pea soup. This persistent and strict diet was occasionally complemented by a bottle of excellent wine from Dülber's cellars. Despite their vulnerability and perpetual fears for their own safety, the prisoners tried not to let their spirits drop. In the best family traditions, and like their relations in Siberia, they performed short scenes and issued their first newspaper *Merry Arnold*, later staging it as a play:

From Xenia to Nicholas II. Dülber.
22nd of March/5th of April, 1918.

My Dear Nicky!.. (M.F.) doesn't write more often because the idea that the letters are read is so unpleasant for her. On the 26th it will be a month since we arrived here...It's already a year since Mama came to the Crimea. The yearning for Ai Todor grows stronger, I'm drawn back there and it seems to me that we aren't even in the Crimea, but in some utterly different place, which only resembles the Crimea, but no more.

...It's sad that they won't let Olga and Irina through, and not entirely understandable.

In Ai Todor...it was terribly uncomfortable. They all turned against us there, and were most unfriendly. I truly don't know what we did to them! It was unpleasant to see how other people's belongings were dealt with, which happens here and there. Here we are more under lock and key than at Ai Todor. The garden is small, with a wall on one side, and the sea on the other, where, by the way, they don't let us go. There's absolutely nowhere to walk...We don't see much of our downstairs neighbours as we all lead our own life. But from time to time I join them downstairs and Mama asks them for tea — or without — each couple to come to us at five o'clock. Too curious that we should be sent up together! Marina and [the original is indecipherable. — Z.B.] ...are very sweet, and we see them every day. The children have become good friends. Spring is very late...

Our house in P. [Petrograd — Z.B.] has also been requisitioned, although we don't know by who in particular and who is living there. I think that very few of the things will remain, as from the day I left, exactly a year tomorrow, there were thefts, pictures went missing, carpets, — and everyone saw how the wine cellar was robbed and its contents carried away (the guards and the steward were held prisoners in a closet while it took place!), and all the silver and linen went missing. A few of our personal servants helped and took part!

...to understand anything of what is taking place is almost impossible. Somebody concluded a peace agreement with G. [Germany — Z.B.], and yet someone is still fighting with the Germans, whilst they continue to move deeper into Russia and have already seized the whole of the Ukraine! It's simply unimaginable...You can see how the noose is being tightened but you don't know how to get out of it. Our poor Russia!

25 M[arch]. My birthday. Alas! I'm forty-three! Today we christened Nadya's little daughter and the whole family was allowed into Tchaer, and Irina and Felix* were allowed to visit us once for two hours. Mama on the whole feels more cheerful, though she hardly gets any fresh air, and has only been on the balcony three times. I don't know when or where we will prepare for Lent. They don't let us into the church. We all tenderly embrace you and love you very dearly. Your old Xenia.[50]

For a period of five months, heavy carts with soldiers and machine-guns, sent by the Yalta Soviet, would pull up at the walls of Dülber and demand that Zadorozhny hand over the Romanovs, threatening to inform Lenin of his counter-revolutionary activities. They advised him to stop playing with the government of the working class, tried to tempt the machine-gunners from the guards over to their side, making calls to their proletarian solidarity. The most absurd instances are described in Sandro's memoirs, such as the setting up, by Zadorozhny, of searchlights, in order to prevent counter-revolutionary generals from stealing the Romanovs away with the help of submarines. Every evening, on his way to sleep, Sandro was not alone in asking them: "So, will you shoot us tonight?"

From Nicholas II to Xenia from Tobolsk.
7th of January, 1918.

...You really cheered me up with your letter and I sincerely thank you for it! It's also a pleasure for us to receive a letter from you. I very much enjoyed the plan for setting up a hotel and the allotment of future functions between you, but will it really be in your house?

It's extremely hard to live without news — telegrams aren't received and sold on the street here every day and they only inform of new horrors and atrocities taking place in our unhappy Russia. It makes one sick to think of how our allies must despise us!

For me — night is the best part of the day, as one can at least forget it all for a while.— The unit committee of our riflemen has just discussed the question of stripping their epaulettes

* Yusupovs.

and other decorations and by a very small majority it was decided not to wear the epaulettes. There were two reasons: first-
ly, their regiments in Ts. Selo had done the same, and secondly,
the attacks of the local soldiers and thugs on riflemen alone in
the streets with the aim of stripping them of their epaulettes.

All the real soldiers, who have spent three years at the front,
were forced to submit to this ridiculous decision in disgust. The
best two companies — of the riflemen regiments — live very
harmoniously. The company of [crossed out] riflemen have
become much worse recently. The relations between them and
the other two are starting to become strained [crossed out].

The same thing is happening everywhere — two or three
nasty ringleaders stir things up and take the rest with them.

Since the New Year the children, with the exception of
Anastasia, have been ill with the German measles, though
they've all got better.

The weather is excellent, it's almost always sunny, and the
frosts are light. I congratulate you on the 24th, dear Xenia.
I heartily embrace you, sweet Mama and everyone else. Christ
be with you!

Sincerely yours,

Nicky.[51]

Sister replying to her brother from Ai Todor.
31st of January.

...Thank God that everyone has recovered and that everything is relatively calm, which can't be said of our abode, where
everything is seething.

Yes, you're absolutely right when you say that night is the
best part of the day, when you can forget everything in your
sleep, and your soul can rest a little. Watching and compre-
hending how our country is being thoughtlessly destroyed
is unbearable, and one simply wonders what the point of living on is! What have they done with our unfortunate people?
Will they ever come to their senses?

Visits from outside have been forbidden, and for the three
months we haven't been allowed to leave Ai Todor. We haven't
seen Irina* since the 6th of January.

* Her daughter, Irina Yusupov.

By the way, several phrases in your letter were crossed out — about the riflemen and their relations (take note!)... it means the letters are being read.

I don't know how we'll survive, everything's so incredibly expensive, and there's no money. We went several days without light, as there was no kerosene. But it's not important, as we'll get by, but it's such a pity for Mama. Why should she suffer and endure all these deprivations and insults at her age?[52]

The food shortages in the Crimea were horrifying. People were literally starving, and at the behest of Soviet deputies there were intensive and widespread searches, and the number of informers giving in information on hidden property increased. A typical document of this era reads: "During a search of the apartment... wine, soap, sugar, gold coins were found... and sent to the children's orphanage and to the quartermaster's commission for soldiers." Later we find another document reading: "The commission presented the guards of Ai Todor, Dülber and Tchaer, the former estates of the grand dukes with: 1 pood 34 pounds of sugar and 3 pounds of tea, for which a signature was received."[53]

On the 12th of March 1918, the Danish Ambassador Harald Skavenius informed his government that the lives of the Imperial family in the Crimea, "under the surveillance of bands of sailors and soldiers", were in danger. "The Dowager Empress, her two daughters and son-in-law, are living under terrible conditions, without money, and experiencing terrible deprivations." On the 3rd of April he again wrote of the total lack of money and shortages of food being experienced by the Crimean captives. The Danish doctor, Carl Krebbs, a representative of the Red Cross, was sent to Yalta with food. Krebbs in vain petitioned Leon Trotsky, the People's Commissar for Foreign Affairs, in an attempt to obtain an exit passport for Marie Feodorovna. "To us, Marie Feodorovna is an old reactionary woman, and her fate is of no interest to us," Trotsky told him, recommending that he submit his petition in the standard manner.[54]

The Romanov hostages had already become the trumps in the card-sharping diplomacy of the Bolsheviks.

Nicholas II to his mother. Tobolsk.
20th of Feb/5th of March, 1918.

My dear sweet Mama,

...More than ever I am with You and dear Xenia, in prayer and in thought, during these most painful times!

The death of Metropolitan Vladimir, my good old general Ivanov, and of Felix* was a great shock to us. Dear Lord! Hasn't enough blood already been spilt! And all these insane killings of officers by people who are allegedly tired of war! Sometimes one really does think that one is going out of one's mind!

One thing is for certain, and that's that whilst Yids are in power things will get worse — what's Russia to them?

The man who was over us here has been at last removed by our soldiers. We only got our dear colonel** who came here with us. He does not read our letters; neither those we get from you; he always brings them himself to pretend before others that things go on as they used to.

In the next few days it will be a year since You came to me in Mogilev, dear Mama! On my knees I thank You for Your goodness and affection then. You gave me comfort and a lift in spirits in those first days — I will <u>never</u> forget that!

Since the 14th of February they have reduced the amounts of our own money that we receive from Petrograd; unfortunately this measure immediately had an effect on our people — we had to dismiss eleven people, as we couldn't afford to pay them all. Many of those who remained with us in the house refused to take their allowances from our personal money, which was very touching. I could write much more, but another time. I tenderly embrace You, sweet beloved Mama. All Benoiton*** send kisses and their love.

Christ be with you!

Yours with all my soul   Nicky.[55]

* Death of Felix was a misinformation.
** Colonel Kobylinsky.
*** Benoiton (French) – in the family circle denoted "your tender, loving" (pl.).

Тобольскъ.   20 Февраля
5 Марта
1918.

Милая дорогая моя Мама,

такъ давно не писалъ

тебѣ, что даже совѣстно

но все боюсь, что письмо

не дойдетъ. Вчера получилъ

письмо отъ Ксеніи и доволь-

но скоро, поэтому сейчасъ

же рѣшилъ написать тебѣ

нѣсколько строкъ.

Болѣе чѣмъ когда-либо, я

съ тобой и милой Ксеніей,

и молитвенно и мысленно,

въ эти тяжелые времена!

Смерть митроп. Владиміра, моего стараго добраго зн. Иванова и потомъ Фрелакса — сильно насъ поразила. Господи! неужели недостаточно крови еще пролито! А всѣ эти безумныя убійства офицеровъ — людей, которые якобы устали отъ войны! Поистинѣ иногда кажется, что сошелъ съ ума! Одно вѣрно, что пока во главѣ будутъ стоять Жиды, все будетъ идти хуже — то имъ Россіи?.

The man who was over us here, has been at last removed

away by our soldiers. We
have only got our dear colonel,
who came here with us. He
does not read our letters;
neither those we get from you:
he always brings them himself
to pretend before others that
things go on as they used to.

Надпись будетъ гоɪ, что
ты прɪѣзжала ко мнѣ въ
Могилевъ, дорогая Мама!
На колѣняхъ благодарю
тебя за твою доброту и ласку
тогда. Ты дала мнѣ
утѣшенiе и бодрость духа
въ тѣ первые дни — никогда
этого не забуду!
Съ 1ɪ февраля сократили намъ
отпускъ нашихъ же денег изъ

Петрограда; къ сожалѣнію эта мѣра сразу отразилась на нашихъ людяхъ — пришлось уволить 11 человѣкъ, за невозможностью платить вебмъ. Многіе, изъ оставшихся съ нами въ домѣ, рѣшительно отказались отъ полученія содержанія изъ нашихъ собствен. денегъ — такъ трогательно. Я могъ бы написать еще много, но лучше до другого раза. — Нѣжно обнимаю тебя, милая любимая Мама. Всѣ Benckton тебя цѣлуютъ и очень любятъ.

Христосъ съ тобой!
Всей душой твой
Ники

Here is how Prince Roman recalls the spring of 1918:

"We were disheartened when we heard of the signing of the peace in Brest-Litovsk. It was unbearable to contemplate that the war, which had cost such sacrifices, had ended so shamefully. Nikolasha didn't acknowledge the treaty, and didn't consider the war to be finished. Amongst the signatures, alongside that of Trotsky, was the name of a certain Ioffe. An Ioffe was the owner of a large restaurant-hall at the railway station in Sevastopol. When the Romanovs arrived in the Crimea and dined in the "Tsar's" Hall, Ioffe would respectfully bow in honour whilst food was being served and would again bow when he was thanked for the good food when they were leaving".[56] Perhaps a certain Adolf Ioffe was from the same family. In May, as the Russian Ambassador in Berlin, he demanded "in the name of the Soviet government that the members of the Tsar's family remain in Russia in order that their lives be saved".[57]

The citrus plants began to turn white, and on the summits of Ai-Petri the snow began to thaw. The elderly sat on the terrace of the castle, whilst the young rambled in the park. Militza visited Minnie daily in a "reception" room, which is to say in her former boudoir, and attempted by any means possible to distract the unhappy mother from thinking of the Imperial family and of her youngest son, Mikhail. Marie Feodorovna became particularly affectionate towards Nikolasha. They often remembered the past with warmth and fondness. Roman became friendly with his cousins, Andrei, Feodor and Nikita. Sandro taught the young boys, having an excellent knowledge of ancient history and Greek mythology in particular. They tried not to think of the future.

In the spring, Prince George Dmitrievich Shervashidze died, the Chamberlain of the household and an old friend of Minnie, who had come to the Crimea in October 1917. He was buried in Koreiz.

Zadorozhny was relatively tactful and attentive in attitude to his prisoners. He took Militza to Yalta himself, in order for her to see Nadya and her first granddaughter Irina. For their safety he moved Nadya and her husband, and Yelena and Stefan Tyshkevich to Tchaer. Olga, Kulikovsky and their son Tikhon lived in Ai Todor, in the building where the wine was stored. Olga Orlova also lived there.

In January 1918 an independent Ukraine sprang up. The Red Army managed to occupy Kiev. Basing themselves in Zhitomir the Ukrainian Rada [council] appealed to the Germans for assistance. Thus the German and Ukrainian offensive began in the South, and in the spring of 1918 the Germans entered the Crimea. In a panic, the Yalta Soviet decided to eliminate the Romanovs and send an armed detachment to besiege Dülber.

As Prince Roman recalled, Zadorozhny proposed that they all move to Alupka and hide in the wine cellars. But the grand dukes decided to "submit themselves to God's will". Zadorozhny returned their personal firearms, hid all their valuables and gold, and then, when the danger had passed, returned all their belongings to them without a single loss. The organisation of the defence of Dülber began under the command of General N.F.Vogel.

They were freed by the Germans! What cruel irony! One fine day a German general appeared in front of the gates of the estate, and explained in French that he was on a mission from the Kaiser to speak "a Sa Majeste L'Imperatrice Marie et au Grand-Duc Nicolas". The mission consisted of inviting the entire family to move to Germany. Minnie and Nikolasha decisively refused the invitation, considering such a move to be a betrayal of their homeland during an unfinished war, as Grand Duke Nicholas did not acknowledge the armistice of the Soviets with Germany*.

On the first day of freedom Tartars appeared and offered to help with the household affairs. The cook, Gromov, finally managed to get to Koreiz and bought provisions. Despite the seasonal fast, there was much gourmandizing and feasting.

---

* Sandro expressed an open interest in the proposal. Minnie informed the German General of her wish to leave for Denmark, but Kaiser Wilhelm refused to use his government as an intermediary.

They sat late into the night in the cosy drawing room. For the first time in many weeks there was no need to stand on guard at the doors and windows with weapons in hand! The next morning a car again appeared from the German command in Yalta. Acting on Nicholas Nikolaevich's orders his proxy, Baron Stahl, announced that the former Supreme Commander and the Empress-Mother had rejected the invitation to leave for Germany. The following morning a German guard-post was set up at the gates to Dülber, but not a single German soldier intruded onto the territory of the estate. In unison they asked the Germans not to prosecute Zadorozhny, who had been captured with other Bolsheviks. The sailor was freed from arrest and allowed to enter Sevastopol. He soon journeyed to Dülber to thank them for their help.[58]

In the spring of 1918, having met with new arrivals from the Caucasus, the Romanovs heard of the political developments, and the formation of the White Army under General Anton Denikin.

In early May, Stana found a buyer for Tchaer, and sold it to an industrialist from the Urals. Now the elder Nikolaevichi, Nadya and her family, and the Tyshkeviches were living in Dülber, and Felix and Irina often visited. In the blue drawing room Felix entertained with his guitar-playing and Russian songs and romances, all sung with an English accent. They often visited Yalta. The Germans enforced order on the city, hotels, shops and restaurants were opened, and on the shore, as in times of peace, citizens could be seen taking promenades. Those who arrived from the North, having endured a host of tragedies, returned to normal life.

On the 26th of May, Xenia, with her family and retinue, returned to Ai Todor. Minnie settled at Kharax with Olga's family. On the 30th of May, Prince Andrei Alexandrovich* married a divorcee, Elizabeth Fabritsievna Sasso-Ruffo**(Elsa), and the ceremony took place in the chapel at Ai Todor.

* The elder son of Sandro and Xenia.
** Her father, an Italian by origin (from the Dukes of Ruffo), was married to Princess Meshcherskaya.

In July they learnt of the murder of the Emperor and his family in Yekaterinburg. They didn't want to believe in such a cruel and horrific event, but the information was soon confirmed. The Empress-Mother alone continued to believe that it was a mistake, and that they were hidden somewhere in Siberia. Soon they received news of the martyr's fate that had fallen on Ella, Sergei Mikhailovich, the Constantinovichi and Vladimir Paley at an abandoned mine shaft near Alapaevsk. Marie Feodorovna asked them all not to pray for the souls of the Emperor's family, as long as she was alive.

September 1918 was marked by the defeat of the German army. On the 29th of October (11 November) 1918 an armistice was signed by Germany and the Entente powers. Towards the end of November an Anglo-French squadron sailed into Novorossiisk. A landing force was then dropped at Sevastopol and Odessa. English and French naval vessels moored up in Sevastopol.

At the end of November, two English ships brought the members of the Family an invitation from the English crown, from the King of Montenegro* and the King of Italy**, to immediately be evacuated. On the 12th of December, Sandro left on an English torpedo boat with his son and Elsa. He headed for Paris with a personal appeal to the Allied leaders, "the Big Four", to give help to the anti-Bolshevik resistance in Russia, and to dispel the widely-held view that things were settling down in Russia and improving. Neither Prime-Minister Clemenceau, nor the other major leaders, received him, and his efforts only led to a meeting with the British Ambassador to France.

They were overjoyed by the possibility of putting an end to their seclusion. Roman, together with Nikita, frequently visited Alupka, where Count Sheremetev and his daughters,

* Prince Nikolai of Montenegro – the father of Militza and Stana, at that stage already the King of Montenegro.
** The Queen of Italy, Helena, was the sister of Militza and Stana.

Praskovia and Maria*, had arrived from the Caucasus, followed by the Countess herself. Alupka belonged to their grand-mother, Countess Vorontsova-Dashkova. In 1921, already in exile abroad, Prince Roman married Countess Praskovia.

In January 1919 they heard of the shooting of the four grand dukes at the Peter and Paul Fortress. The situation on the fronts in the first months of 1919 gave much hope to the Romanovs: Denikin's army had moved forward into the North, and Admiral Kolchak had great successes in Siberia on his route to the Volga. On the Southern front, after the Germans had left the Ukraine, the Red Army's advance began. But the fervent nationalist Petlura seized power on the 13th of November 1918, and threw the Bolsheviks out of Kiev. Petlura armed the peas-ants, and under the banner of civil war, maraudered and killed in those regions that didn't acknowledge his authority. Pet-lura's forces captured the towns of Kherson and Nikolaev. However, in the beginning of January 1919, the Red Army cleared the territory of the Ukraine with the assistance of re-belling peasants under the command of Ataman Grigoriev.

Towards the end of 1919, the Allied central command in Constantinople, which represented the governments of Great Britain, France, Greece, Italy and the United States, decided that the Northern coast of the Black Sea, together with the port of Odessa and the Southern Crimea, should become the responsibility of the French. France announced its readiness to defend Odessa and the Crimea from the Bolsheviks. But in March 1919 there was a mutiny on the French ships, and the sailors received a promise from their admiral that they would be sent home. As a result the French began to secretly remove their forces from Odessa, in the process leaving the Volun-teer Army to the mercy of fate. They hurriedly evacuated the

---

* Praskovia's family left Petrograd in March 1917 for the Kuskovo estate near Moscow, and in the summer, together with Countess Vorontsova-Dashkova, moved to *Mineralnye Vody* ("Mineral Waters") and Yessentuki. The Sheremetevs, the Count and the elder son Sergei hid from the Bolsheviks in the mountains, and made it to the Crimea through Yekaterinodar.

area, and in early April the Red Army entered the Crimea and reached the Perekop Isthmus, which joins the Crimea to the mainland.

Those who did not sympathise with the Bolsheviks were panic-stricken. Yalta was the last remaining corner of Imperialist Russia. Via Kerch and Novorossiisk, many fled from the Crimea to the Kuban region, which remained the territory of the White Army right up until the defeat of General Wrangel in 1920.

In February 1919, the English sea command again proposed that the Dowager leave the Crimea. Minnie hesitated, not wishing to leave the Russian land, as she was convinced that the presence of the Empress near Yalta, together with the other members of the Family, would strengthen the fighting spirit of the defenders of the monarchy. She could not be convinced to leave Kharax. She announced that she would remain until she received a guarantee that all those in her entourage who so wished could also leave the Crimea.

Vice-Admiral Hon. Sir S. Gough-Calthorpe, the British High Commissioner and Naval Commander-in-Chief, based in Constantinople, sent his largest naval ship, the H.M.S. *Marlborough*, to Sevastopol. The ship's Captain, Johnson, arrived at Kharax with a letter from the Queen-Mother, Alexandra. His accounts of what the English in Sevastopol had heard and seen had a strong effect on the Crimean captives: of sunken ships, the atrocities inflicted on officers, who were burnt alive or thrown overboard with weights tied to their legs.

Marie Feodorovna agreed to leave on condition that she could take all her relations and their retainers. The Nikolaevichi in Dülber began to pack their things. Olga and Kulikovsky decided to leave for the Caucasus. Sergei Duke of Leuchtenberg announced his departure for Sevastopol, and his intention to join the Allied Powers fleet.

Having returned to Sevastopol after his talks with the Empress, the Captain commanded that the *Marlborough* take course for Yalta, in order to take on board those passengers that Her Majesty wished to accompany her. The British sailors met with an unexpected problem: the number of passengers to be taken on board was greater than had been estimated when the ship had been sent on its mission. They had only allowed for the Empress and her close friends and relatives that amounted or ten to twelve people. Now they had to provide food and shelter for a vast number. All thirty-five of the officers' cabins were freed, and two or three beds were put in each. Without difficulty thirty mattresses were found, although sheets quickly became a luxury. The Captain's cabin was set aside for the Empress. Marie refused to board the ship from the pier in Yalta, and so the *Marlborough* entered the bay at Koreiz, very close to Kharax. With the aid of an improvised pier, forty passengers were taken on board, amongst whom there were many women and five children aged from one to six. Many of the passengers who boarded on the first evening, on the 7th of April, had only been informed an hour before their departure, and arrived only with hand-baggage. But late into the evening a huge quantity of baggage arrived, literally measurable in tons, without labels or with name-tags in Russian. Only the Empress's few small cases showed her monogram. The baggage could have become confused, were it not for excellent English of Princess Marina Petrovna.[59]

H.M.S.*Marlborough* left Koreiz, but again dropped anchor not far from Yalta, in order to take on board another group of passengers, of whom thirty-eight were women. The inhabitants of Dülber arrived: the families of Peter, Nikolasha and Stana, the Tyshkeviches, the Yusupovs, the Dolgorukies, Olga Orlova and their retinues. Grand Duke Nicholas, the former Viceroy of the Caucasus, appeared in a Circassian coat and Astrakhan *papakha* (a Caucasian fur cap). Prince Yusupov Sr., once the governor of Moscow, also appeared in a Circassian coat. With him left his wife, Zinaida, his son Felix, his daughter-in-law Irina, and "Baby Rina", his six-year old granddaughter.

Xenia left with her five sons; Prince Feodor was twenty, and the youngest, Vassili, was twelve. The youngsters, particularly Vassili, were excited by the prospect of a trip on the warship.

The H.M.S. *Marlborough* set something of a record: for two weeks it was inhabited by women representing four generations of the Imperial family – Minnie, Xenia, Irina Yusupova, and little Rina.

"I cannot end my account of this first day of the embarkation without mentioning the extraordinary fortitude shown by these people on their day of severance from their country. For fifteen months many of them had been in constant danger of assassination, and even now none of them could have had a clear picture of their future. Though it seemed likely that the Empress Marie and those closest to her would go to England for a time, the destination of the remainder was not then known. Nevertheless, their chief concern was to cause us as little inconvenience as possible. They expressed repeatedly their gratitude for the little we were able to do in providing for their comfort, while declaring that they had been prepared to be satisfied with much less."[60]

On the following day, the 8th of April, the last travelling companions of Her Majesty, and tons of baggage were taken on board, which had to be loaded not only by the English sailors, but by a shoreline detachment of one hundred and twenty officers from the Imperial Army. Every morning on the deck the little ceremony was daily observed. Nikolasha, with stately dignity, would approach the Empress, who would already be sitting in an armchair on deck, and presented himself to her, giving his faultless military salute, and paid her courtly and graceful homage, by bending low and kissing her hand.

On the 11th of April 1919, they left Yalta. All the passengers watched, watery-eyed, as the thin strip of shoreline disappeared into the distance. At that stage they didn't realise that they were leaving Russia forever, and that the dynasty that had ruled since 1613 had come to an end. They all deeply and naively believed in the innate loyalty of the Russian people to their sovereigns, in their attachment to religion, customs and traditions. The cruiser set course for Constantinople. There were eighty-five passengers on board, including twenty members of the Imperial family, among them two children, and twenty-five members, of both sexes, of the retinues of Her Majesty and Their Highnesses, and their servants. And two hundred tons of luggage.

During the two-day journey to Constantinople the Empress rarely left her cabin. The overwhelming feeling was that of having been saved from a shipwreck. It was noticed that for the first time in a year Xenia could be seen smiling. Only Felix Yusupov took it all as an adventure. This Oxford graduate quickly became a favourite of the crew, recounted the events of the assassination of Rasputin, played the balalaika and brilliantly performed Gypsy romances to a guitar accompaniment. Felix had managed to bring two paintings by Rembrandt from the priceless family collection held at the celebrated Yusupov Palace on the Moika Canal in Petersburg. Roman Petrovich wrote in his memoirs of the long parcel with which Felix could not be parted on the first evening on deck of the ship. He showed one canvas to Roman. Later, both paintings were sold by the Yusupovs in America.

The Nikolaevichi received an invitation that had been passed on from the Italian King, offering them the chance to transfer ships at Constantinople, and to travel on to Genoa. On the 16th of April, Nikolasha and Peter, with their wives, Roman, Marina and another twenty passengers, transferred onto the H.M.S. *Lord Nelson*. The morning was spent unloading and reloading the luggage of the grand dukes, which consisted of over two hundred heavy cases, as they had managed to bring away a great quantity of silver, and possibly gold plate. On bidding farewell to the officers of the ship, Nikolasha unsheathed his Sword of Honour with its old Damascus blade, the hilt of which was encrusted with priceless diamonds. The scabbard itself was decorated with smaller gemstones. He had received the sabre as a gift from the Emperor following the victory of the Russian forces in Galicia. This opulent masterpiece had been wrapped in a grimy piece of wash-leather, and had survived through numerous searches.

In Constantinople they parted. Marie Feodorovna and her family journeyed on to Malta. A telegram was waiting for her from King George V, inviting her to London. But the British Government, however, refused domicile in England to all except the Dowager Empress, Xenia, and a few of their respective suites and retainers. There was a fear in London that the revolutionary squall that had shaken the thrones of the Romanovs, the Hapsburgs, and the Hohenzollerns, might shake the sturdy foundations of the House of Windsor. Thus, far from Russia, the members of the family found themselves separated from one another. Many would only meet again at funerals, which were not long coming.

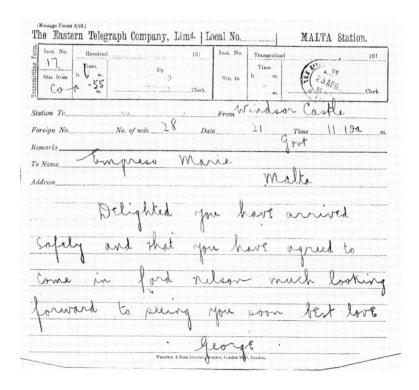

Epilogue

Again the Romanovs found themselves scattered. The Dowager Empress Marie settled in her homeland, in Copenhagen, in the King's Amalienborg Castle, in the same wing where her father, Christian IX's apartments had been situated. Her intensely frugal nephew, Christian X, argued with his aunt, even about the electricity bill. To the relief of the Danish King, in 1920, Marie Feodorovna moved to the Hvidore Castle, which she had bought with her two sisters in 1907. In Denmark she was considered a legendary figure who had endured a multitude of tragic events. The Empress Marie died in 1928, at the age of eighty-one, and all the Romanovs gathered for her funeral, setting family disputes and squabbles aside. Her remains lie in the Royal burial vault at Roskilde in Denmark.

Whilst still on board the *Marlborough*, the Grand Dukes Nicholas and Peter decided that they would leave incognito whilst abroad, taking the name Borisov (from the name of the estate which they jointly owned), and that they would not become involved in politics. Nikolasha moved from Italy to France, remaining in rank the most senior and most respected of the eight grand dukes that survived the Bolshevik executions. Many of the émigré community believed that he would lay claim to the title of Head of the Family and to the crown. But the Supreme Monarchist Council didn't officially put forward his candidacy for leadership of the monarchical organization. It is known that Nikolasha in no uncertain terms condemned the actions of Cyril Vladimirovich, who in 1924 declared himself "The Tsar of Russia", Emperor Kirill I, the Head of the Dynasty and the pretender to the throne of all the Russias. The son of a Lutheran mother, he had twice broken his vow to his sovereign: first by his actions in the State Duma, even before Nicholas II had abdicated, and secondly by renouncing all claims to the throne in a document of the 3rd of March 1917, albeit at the insistence of the Provisional Government. He had conducted himself immorally when in haste he left Petrograd in the spring of 1917, being the only grand duke to escape Russia for good when his sovereign was still under arrest. For Nikolasha such a be-haviour of the self-styled Emperor was impermissible, if only because the Dowager Empress was still alive in Copenhagen, where she continued to refuse to believe that both her sons had died, and never acknowledged Cyril's title. Nikolasha kept a verbal agreement made between the eight grand dukes who had found themselves in exile.

It is possible that the Grand Duke's reluctance stemmed from his considerable age, sickness, waning strength, and the fact that he didn't have an heir. He died in Cap d'Antibes in January 1929, and his funeral became a magnificent ceremonial affair, in which the government of France took part: the French hadn't forgotten that during the First World War, their loyal and experienced ally was the Commander-in-Chief of the Russian army. Anastasia Nikolaevna outlived her husband by six years, and died in Antibes in 1935.

Peter Nikolaevich lived near his brother, also in France, and in 1931 he too passed away in Antibes. In his final years he lived alone, and occupied himself with historical and religious painting. In 1936 his widow and children moved to Italy, under the patronage of Queen Helena. When the Germans occupied Italy, Grand Duchess Militza hid in the Vatican, while the other members of the family hid with their Roman friends. Later the family moved to Egypt, where Militza Nikolaevna died in Alexandria in 1951. King Faruk sent his representatives to her funeral. Her coffin, covered in the Russian national flag, was carried by Russians, before being sent to Cannes.

Xenia and Sandro had separated long before the revolution, and in emigration they lived apart in different countries. Alexander Mikhailovich preferred France and the USA, living out his final years in Paris, where he died in 1933. At first Xenia settled with her mother in Denmark, before returning to England, where George V gave her the use of a comfortable house, Frogmore, close to Windsor. King Edward VIII offered her a house at Hampton Court, in the suburbs of London, where Grand Duchess Xenia passed away in 1960, surrounded by her adoring grandsons. Her sister, Grand Duchess Olga, died in the same year in Canada. In the first years of emigration, Olga and her family had lived in the Hvidore Castle, and for a number of years Kulikovsky managed a stable for a millionaire. Their sons, Tikhon and Gury, went on to serve in the Danish Guards. In 1948, Olga and her husband and children moved to Canada. Old age, sickness and poverty carried the parents to their graves.

The six sons of Xenia and Sandro all married representatives of aristocratic Russian families. Prince Feodor married Princess Irina Pavlovna*, and their son Mikhail Feodorovich lives in Paris and has visited Russia a number of times. Prince Nikita Alexandrovich married Countess Maria Vorontsova-Dashkova, and they lived in New York, where they had two sons. Prince Dmitry married Countess Maria Golenishcheva-Kutuzova, and they had a daughter, Nadezhda. Prince Rostislav's first marriage was to Princess Alexandra Golitsyna, and his second was to Alice Baker. Prince Vassili married Princess Natalia Golitsyna, and their daughter, Marina, visited St. Petersburg in 1997.

Felix and Irina Yusupov, whilst their means permitted them, lived in luxury in the most beautiful cities of Europe and America. Felix died in 1967 at the age of eighty, and was mourned by his relations and hundreds of friends. Irina passed away three years later, and was buried next to her husband and father-in-law at the Saint-Genevieve-de-Bois cemetery. The former passenger of the *Marlborough*, baby Rina, married Prince Nicholas Sheremetev, and died in 1983. Their daughter, Xenia Sfirits, and her daughter Tatiana (born 1968), Felix's great-granddaughter, prefer to live in Greece.

A friendship has lasted since their childhood years amongst the grandchildren of Xenia and Peter Nikolaevich, – Nicholas Romanovich Romanov, Nikita and Alexander Nikitich Romanov, and Mikhail Feodorovich Romanov. They are the main participants in the Family Union of the Romanovs in our era. Their wish is to bring aid to Russia, and not to make use of her and her long-suffering people.

* Irina Paley.

REFERENCES

1 *Krymski vestnik*, No.71, 19 March, 1917 (*The Crimean Herald*)
2 R.Romanow, p.405
3 ibid, p.407
4 *Yuzhnye vedomosti*, No.65, 21.03.1917 (*The Southern Gazette*)
5 Passion, p.556
6 *Krymski vestnik*, No.69, 17.03.1917 (*The Crimean Herald*)
7 *Dnevniki* (*Diaries*), p.585
8 Hoover, box 1, *fond* 16
9 *Dnevniki* (*Diaries*), p.585
10 Hoover, box 1, *fond* 16
11 ibid
12 ibid, box 2, *fond* 2
13 Passion, p.552
14 Hoover, box 2, *fond* 2
15 ibid
16 Hoover, box 6, *fond* 12
17 ibid, *fond* 2
18 A.M., p.234
19 ibid, p.235
20 ibid
21 ibid, p.236
22 Hoover, box 7, *fond* 1
23 *Yaltinskaya Zhizn'*, 4 August, 1917 (*The Yalta Life*)
24 Hoover, box 7, *fond* 1
25 R.Romanow, p.410
26 *Izvestia…*, No. 29, 16 May, 1917 (*The News of the Tavrichesky Regional Social Committee*)
27 A.M., p.236
28 Hoover, box 7, *fond* 1
29 R.Romanow, p.408
30 Hoover, box 7, *fond* 1
31 *Yuzhnye vedomosti*, 24 April, 1917 (*The Southern Gazette*)
32 A.M., p.239
33 Hoover, box 7, *fond* 1
34 R.Romanow, p.410,411
35 ibid, p.412–414
36 *Izvestia…*, 30.04.1917 (*The News of the Tavrichesky…*)
37 ibid, 22.06.1917
38 *Krymski vestnik*, 22.06.1917 (*The Crimean Herald*)
39 ibid, 14.09.1917
40 ibid
41 Perchonok, p.198
42 R.Romanow, p.408
43 *Krymski vestnik*, No. 213, 14 Sep., 1917 (*The Crimean Herald*)
44 Kudrina, p.53
45 *Krymsky vestnik*, No. 213 (*The Crimean Herald*)
46 ibid
47 Hoover, box 6, *fond* 6
48 ibid
49 Passion, p.592
50 Hoover, box 6, *fond* 6
51 ibid
52 Passion, p.603
53 *Vol'ny yug*, 27.01.1918 (*The Free South*)
54 Kudrina, p.53
55 Hoover, box 6, *fond* 6
56 R.Romanow, p.422
57 Kudrina, p.53
58 R.Romanow, p.429
59 Pridham, p.68
60 ibid, p.69

Bibliography

Russian Language Sources:

Alexander Mikhailovich, velikii kniaz: *Kniga vospominanii*, Moscow–Leningrad, 1991

Belyakova, Zoia: *Nikolaevsky Dvorets*, St.Petersburg, 1997

Bogdanovich A.V.: *Dnevnik*, Moscow–Leningrad, 1924

Bokhanov A.: *"Obrechionnyi"*, in *Rodina*, 1994, No.5, p.42–47

Buranov Yu., Khrustalev V. *Gibel' Imperatorskogo Doma*, Moscow, 1992

Dnevniki imperatora Nikolaia II, Moscow, 1991

Yepanchin N.A.: *Na sluzhbe trekh imperatorov,* Moscow, 1996

Zhiliar P.: *Imperator Nikolai II i ego semia*, Vienna, 1921 (reprint)

Lamzdorf V.N.: *Dnevnik V.N.Lamzdorfa* (1886–1890), Moscow–Leningrad, 1926

Kudrina, Julia: *"Ty molishsia o svoyom bednom Niki"*, in *Rodina*, 1997, No.8

Mosolov A.A.: *Pri dvore poslednego imperatora*, St.Petersburg, 1992

Oldenburg S.S.: *Tsarstvovanie imperatora Nikolaya II*, St.Petersburg, 1991

Perchonok F.: *Milaya obozhaemaya Anna Vasilievna*, Moscow, 1996

Polovtsov A.A.: *Dnevnik Gosudarstvennogo Sekretaria*, vol.1-2, Moscow, 1966

Popova G.: *Osobniak grafini Karlovoi*, St.Petersburg, 1996

Radzinski E. *Gospodi... spasi i usmiri Rossiiu*, Moscow, 1993

Romanovy i Krym, Moscow, 1993

Shestakov I.: *Dnevniki, 1882–1887*. CGA VMF, *fond* 26

Shumigorski E.S.: *Imperatorskoe zhenskoe patrioticheskoe obshchestvo*, St.Petersburg, 1912

Scott, Staffan: *Romanovy. Kto oni?* Yekaterinburg, 1993

Tolstaia A.A.: *Zapiski freiliny*, Moscow, 1996

Tiutcheva A.F.: *Pri dvore dvukh imperatorov*, Moscow, 1990 (Dnevnik. 1929)

Tseliad M.P.: *Dvorets Belosselskikh-Belozerskikh*, St.Petersburg, 1996

Valuev P.A.: *Dnevnik P.A.Valueva, ministra vnutrennikh del*, vol.1-2, Moscow, 1961

Voeikov V.N.: *S tsarem i bez tsaria*, Moscow, 1960

Volkonski S.M.: *Moi vospominaniia*, Moscow, 1992

Witte S.Yu.: *Vospominaniia*, vol.1-3, Moscow, 1969

Selected Bibliography

Almedingen E.M.: *An Unbroken Unity: A Memoir of Grand Duchess Sergei*, London, 1964

Belyakova, Zoia: *Grand Duchess Maria Nikolaevna and Her Palace in St. Petersburg*, St.Petersburg, 1996

Crawford, Rosemary and Donald: *Michail and Natasha*, London, 1997

Chavchavadze, David, prince: *The Grand Dukes*, New York, 1990

Historish-genealogishes Handbuch über alle Linien des hohen Regentenhauses, Hessen. Marburg, 1874

King, Greg: *The Last Empress*, New York, 1996

Kurth, Peter: *The Tsar,* Boston, New York,Toronto, London, 1995

Lieven, Domenic: *Nicholas II,* London, 1993

Mager, Hugo: *Elizabeth Grand Duchess of Russia*, New York, 1998

Massie, R.: *Nicholas and Alexandra*, New York, 1967

Marie (Pavlovna), Grand Duchess: *Education of a Princess*, New York, 1931

Maylunas A., Mironenko S.: *A Lifelong Passion*, London, 1996

Paleologue, Maurice: *An Ambassador's Memoirs*, London, 1922

Pridham, Sir Francis, *Close of a Dynasty*, London, 1956

Romanow, Roman, Prinz: *Am Hof des Letzen Zaren*, München-Zürich, 1995

Russian Court Memoirs. B.M., London, 1917

Yusupov, Prince Felix: *Lost Splendor*, London, 1953

Vorres, Ian: *The Last Grand Duchess*, New York, 1965

Archives, Private papers

Arkhiv FSB (NKVD), No.1433

Arkhiv Rossiiskoi Natsionalnoi Biblioteki (Archives of the Russian National Library). Lichnoe delo D.E.Leuchtenberg, without No.

RGIA, *fond* 468 (State Archives of the Russian Federation, Moscow)

RGIA, *opis'* 431/1565, *opis'* 432/1566

RGIA, *opis'* 501/2191

RGA VMF, *fond* 26 (Rossiiskii gosudarstvennyi arkhiv voenno-morskogo flota)

Kseniia Aleksandrovna, Grand Duchess of Russia. Correspondence (1904– 1929). Diaries (1916–1919). Hoover Institution Archives, Stanford University. USA

Abbreviations used in References

A.M. – Grand Duke Alexander Mikhailovich

Hoover – Hoover Institution Archives, Stanford University, CA, USA

M.P., Education – Marie (Pavlovna), Grand Duchess. *Education of a Princess*

Passion – Maylunas, Mironenko. *A Lifelong Passion*

RGIA – Rossiiskii Gosudarstvennyi Istoricheskii Arkhiv, St.Petersburg

CONTENTS

ZOIA BELYAKOVA

THE ROMANOVS.
The Way It Was

EGO Publishers

8 Gorokhovaya St.,
191186, St. Petersburg,
Russia
Tel. (812) 315-2773
fax (812) 312-9284

Licence No. 040054 LR
from 22.08.96